THE POWER
OF
THE CROSS

THE POWER OF THE CROSS

OF

THE CROSS

*Foundations for a
Christian Feminist Ethic
of Community*

SALLY B. PURVIS

ABINGDON PRESS
Nashville

THE POWER OF THE CROSS:
FOUNDATIONS FOR A CHRISTIAN FEMINIST ETHIC OF COMMUNITY

Copyright © 1993 by Abingdon Press

This book is printed on recycled, acid-free paper.

Library of Congress Cataloging-in-Publication Data

Purvis, Sally B., 1945-
    The power of the cross : foundations for Christian feminist ethnic of community / Sally B. Purvis.
        p.   cm.
    Includes bibliographical references.
    ISBN 0-687-33206-0 (alk. paper)
    1. Power (Christian theology) 2. Feminist theology. 3. Feminism—Moral and ethical aspects. I. Title.
BT738.25.P87   1993
230'.082—dc20   92-41372
                                                                                          CIP

Scripture quotations are from the New Revised Standard Version Bible, Copyright 1989 by the Division of Christian Education of the National Council of the Churches of Christ in the USA. Used by permission.

93 94 95 96 97 98 99 00 01 02 — 10 9 8 7 6 5 4 3 2 1

To Norfield Congregational Church, Weston, Connecticut. The community there taught me a great deal about power as control and showed me more than I could imagine about power as life and love.

CONTENTS

ACKNOWLEDGMENTS

The project of producing this book has been a long one, starting with the formulation and writing of my doctoral dissertation. My first thank yous, then, belong to Richard B. Hays and Margaret A. Farley, who patiently and insightfully guided me through that process with more love than control.

I also want to thank my colleagues at Candler School of Theology for their support and to the institution for the break from teaching that allowed relatively uninterrupted writing time.

I want to include a special thank you to Tom Milazzo, who read the whole manuscript, and to my editor at Abingdon Press, Ulrike Guthrie, who supplied helpful suggestions and midcourse corrections.

A final and personal thank you to GROUP for always being there and to Judy for the warmth and freedom I needed to complete this.

INTRODUCTION

THE ISSUES AND THE ARGUMENT

Power. When we think of power, images fly through our consciousness with kaleidoscopic intensity and diversity. Some are comforting images from childhood: caring adults rescuing your kitten from a tree. Other old images can still provoke fear: adult faces angry, voices shouting, fists raised. We have distant memories of our own power and its absence, the things we could do well and that brought esteem, and of course the things that remained beyond our ability to manipulate them: machines, numbers, words, our own bodies at times. From our young adulthood we may have images of trying to navigate a world we knew little about and were concentrating our whole being on learning. And there are more current images, pictures that flash through our minds like *Life* magazine photos—of military power and its consequences; of world leaders, white men in dark suits; of Wall Street, its building and intangible structures. There are more personal images, dances of relationships, as we move well or poorly together and sometimes do not stay connected at all, fitting and not fitting into institutional structures—families, work, politics, economics, church, all of them. In this horizontally and vertically mobile society, we continue to see images of navigating more new worlds, across class and race and ethnic lines, worlds we know something about but in which we have to watch our footing in order to keep our balance.

All of these images, and the myriad others that provide the

texture of our consciousness, have something to do with power. I begin my discussion with images rather than definitions because I believe that our "knowledge" of the nature and function of power in any given setting is as much a function of our imagination and intuition as it is of our "pure rationality."[1] Our sense of power—what it is, who has it, where it comes from—is part of our fundamental orientation toward reality. To return to a metaphor, it is the drum beat of the dance of our relationships, the background rhythm against which, to which, we move together. This sense of power that we move to is not exactly unconscious, but it is often assumed, unarticulated, part of what "goes without saying."[2] It is an aspect of the shared assumptions that hold together these worlds that we learn and help to shape.

Any attempt to reorder relationships, be they internal, between two people, communal, institutional, national, or international, must take account of the images of power that are part of the assumed reality. If the fundamental image of power is unchanged, then many of the fundamental features of the relationship will also remain the same. Radical change, change that goes to the root of the matter, will also involve a change in the shared understanding and implementation of power.

Radical change in relational and communal structures constitutes at least part of the project of all contemporary Christian feminists. Moving beyond the white, middle-class, liberal goals of the early 1960s, white feminists in the 1980s and 1990s have excavated more and more levels of oppression, internal as well as external, in an attempt to find ways to structure human society so that all persons can flourish.[3] The closer we get to the roots, the more we encounter issues of power, assumptions that must be spoken, changes that must be made. We cannot hope to reconstitute social relations in ways that enact new values and insights about old values if we leave untouched, unchanged the predominant assumptions and practices of power with which our society operates.

For a Christian feminist, or at least for this Christian feminist, the contemporary enterprise of reenvisioning and reimaging power in order to create new communal realities carries with it a sense of *déjà vu*. Radical reordering of community based upon a radical reinterpretation of the nature and function of power strikes me as an accurate description of the work of the earliest Christian communities insofar as we can discern them through the documents we have to examine. It was precisely the shared assumptions about power—God's power, human power, institutional power, what "everyone knew" in the first-century Roman Empire—that were challenged by the life, death, and resurrection of Jesus Christ. And it was the new understanding of power, the power of the cross, that was, for a while, the heartbeat of the new communal life that was being formed. For a small group of people, the life, death, and resurrection of Jesus the Christ overturned, undermined, and reshuffled a whole panoply of cultural assumptions, values, descriptions of what the world is "really like," including assumptions about the nature of power. This new understanding of power, the power of the cross, is articulated most clearly in Paul's first letter to the community at Corinth, but it is present as well in his other letters and to some degree in the Gospels and Acts. A great cultural, communal experiment began, albeit on a small scale: the enactment of a "new world" to live out the new vision of reality that the early Christians claimed to have seen, to see.[4]

Very soon, at least by the time of the Pastoral Epistles, the "new world" began to look remarkably like the old one had looked, with institutional structures assuming oppressive, hierarchical forms.[5] By the fourth century, when the emperor Constantine baptized Christianity with political respectability, very little if anything remained of the radical reordering of human community based on the power of the cross. In the intervening centuries, there have been experimental pockets of communal restructuring, but by and large the Christian church(es) has operated with an understanding of power that is not based on, or in harmony with, the power of the cross as articulated in the earliest Christian documents.[6] We seem to have lost our center, to have forgotten our roots.

Contemporary Christian feminist scholarship can be read in part as an attempt to recover the center, to expose the roots, of Christian community as it digs at the foundations of relationships and institutions that are oppressive to individuals and groups, including feminist relationships and institutions.[7] It invites us to return to the insights and structures of early Christian communal experiments, even though those experiments never succeeded in ways that we hope for today. It also demands that we take account of the experiences of the intervening centuries and move our communal ethics in directions that the first Christians could not possibly have envisioned and articulated. That is, it not only reinterprets but also in some ways expands the "canon."[8]

Contemporary feminists, including Christian feminists, have been wary of the cross as a symbol for community. As several scholars have cogently and persuasively argued, the cross has been used to justify, even glorify, suffering in ways that are damaging to persons.[9] It has also distorted persons' understanding of responsibility, guilt, sin—that is, the cross is theologically and ethically dangerous.

There is no doubt that the cross has functioned as an instrument of violence—spiritual, psychological, physical—from the first century onward.[10] However, I will argue that it can only be used to harm and oppress within certain shared assumptions and practices of power, and that, properly understood, the "power of the cross" subverts its own nature as harmful and oppressive and becomes instead an intellectual, spiritual, and communal resource for radical change.

CONTEMPORARY EXCAVATION

The deconstructive project of Christian feminist ethics is well underway. For the last twenty-five years we have been learning to see and to name the powers and forces, the structures and practices that oppress women. We have been developing a language that both connects with and departs from traditional Christian languages. We have examined our resources, both those within and those outside of Christianity, and have been evaluating their usefulness for new understandings and embodiments of Christian community. We have critiqued and added to what counts as "canon." We have articulated and communicated insights regarding perspectives from which we view the world, including God and ourselves, and we have expanded those insights as the conversation extends to more and more persons. In short, we have gotten very good at identifying the problems.

Part of what we have been learning in this process of excavating the layers of oppression, and in examining the various forms and textures it may have, is the complexity and intractability of the structures that oppress. Each new layer that we uncover seems to expose another; it is possible to experience a kind of lethargy and/or impatience in the face of our suspicion that there is no end to the digging. Thus we hear cries of "enough deconstruction; it is time to start building." Those cries come from the classroom, the churches, and the depths of our own hearts. Even the oppressors begin to demand that we stop pointing out what is wrong and start doing things better.

Of course, in many instances, we have started doing things better. In our culture, women and women's issues are now taken far more seriously than they were at the start of this wave of the women's movement, both outside of and within Christian communities. In some cases, women's issues and social issues have started to look the same. Even the strength of the resistance to women's liberation is some testimony to the seriousness with which it is addressed.[11] We have begun to experiment with other communal visions, new possibilities, often though not always on the fringes of mainstream society.

However, although I share the impatience with the deconstructive process and have a yearning to move on, this book is as deconstructive as it is reconstructive. I will continue the digging as I concentrate on yet another layer of oppression, that of the level of power in community, and I will discuss what is wrong as extensively as how to improve it. The conceptualization and implementation of power is such a fundamental aspect of communal structure that without addressing it, true, lasting change is impossible. Any building that we construct on the foundation of power with which we are the most familiar will not be a radically new structure but rather a revision of the old one, somewhat altered, but fundamentally the same. We need to begin our reconstruction at the base, and the base is power.

One of the more frustrating aspects of being involved in feminist groups is the extent to which, for all of the revolutionary rhetoric, they mimic the very oppressive structures they seek to overcome. Commitments to cooperate degenerate into attempts to dominate, the common good is lost in cliques, horizontal violence abounds as the powerless attack one another, and the most commonly shared experience can be a sense of betrayal. Similar frustrations and pain are often experienced in attempts to construct Christian communities that are to some extent countercultural. Part of the failure to enact anything really new can be attributed to the difficulty of change. The old way is always easier, even if it is more painful and destructive. However, part of the problem is that groups try to create new communities on the old power base, and the change does not go deeply enough to permeate the rest of the structure. The same old dynamics creep back into the most well-meaning relationships, and the correctives both in terms of insights into the problem and concrete attempts to solve it do not work.

Reenvisioning and reenacting power will not of themselves make communal transformation easy. In addition to the difficulty inherent in the process of change itself, even change that is desirable and intended, we are all shaped by the old power structures, tied to whatever privilege they may afford, limited in our imagination and energy. Furthermore, we are not always well-meaning.

Nonetheless, it is my conviction, and to some limited extent my experience, that when the understanding and practice of power can be transformed, truly new possibilities can exist for Christian community; the power of the cross continues to be revelatory. It is that revelation that I am concerned to develop as a step toward shaping our lives together in enriching and fulfilling ways.

PERSPECTIVE AND LIMITATIONS

This is a book about ethics; it is about the understandings and guidelines and structures for being and doing that are more conducive to good human life. It has, however, a very limited focus: the nature and practice of power. In this light, I will examine and discuss the foundations for communal ethics; structuring the edifice itself is another project.

I am a Christian writing for persons interested in resources and ethical structures for Christian community. I will leave to others questions about its more general relevance. I am also middle-income and white, and I address the issue of power, Christian understandings and practices of power, from the perspective of the privileged. I write from and to churches that are primarily white and middle-income and whose experiences of power outside the church structure are to a large degree characterized by privilege, however powerless individual persons may feel. This is my social location, and I believe that the conversation about power among the privileged, at least among the privileged who call themselves Christian, is a conversation we need to have.

I draw heavily upon personal experience in my analysis, my own and that of my reader. Without some shared experiences of the nature and practice of power, much of what I seek to evoke may be simply unavailable. Since I write from a position of social privilege, I cannot assume that my discussion of power will touch the experience of those whose lives are characterized by structural powerlessness. That is not to say that the "power of the weak" is not real.[12] Rather, it is only to say that our understanding and experience of power will be shaped to a large extent by our place in the social order.

White Christian female feminists have the ongoing experience of being both privileged and disadvantaged, powerful in social terms and powerless. It may be the discontinuities of our experience that have highlighted the centrality of the issue of power for the project of structuring our lives together in new ways that avoid the oppression of which we are both victims and agents. White Christian feminists have deeply influenced my thought, and it is they who are my primary dialogue partners in this analysis and revisioning of power.

One final personal note: I came to feminism and Christianity at the same time in my life, and I have consistently heard the message of feminism and the message of the gospel as fundamentally the same. I realize that this does not represent common experience, either of feminist or of nonfeminist Christians. What my experience enables me to do is to hear resonances between the two with a clarity and at a volume that may not be generally accessible. However, it also makes it difficult at times for me to hear clearly those who understand the two to be in irreconcilable conflict. Thus I write from a perspective of the coherence of a Christian feminist position and may not always address issues that seem incongruent to others.

DIRECTIONS OF THE ETHIC

In the first two chapters I will define and illustrate the two conceptions of power that I see at work in our culture as well as in the history of Christianity. One I will term "power as control," the other as "power as life." In chapter 3 I will offer a conceptual map of four dimensions of power, discussing at each level and at the interactions among them the "different worlds" that emerge from the two different conceptions of power. Chapter 4 will be the bridge between the early Christian communities and contemporary Christian feminists' insights regarding the nature of power and its embodiment in human communities. In chapter 5 I will sketch some of the fundamental normative structural features of cruciform community as I have described it, and the final chapter will draw together the arguments and suggest some directions for future conversations.

ONE FACE OF POWER: POWER AS CONTROL

S omewhere beneath our conscious awareness but available for our conscious retrieval and examination are our experiences and understandings of power. When the subject matter of our discussion is so closely tied to our experience, we need to bring that experience to consciousness so that the abstractions we use to talk about it are connected with our lives. Issues of power are at the root of our attempts to understand and structure healthy human community, whatever the specific normative shape(s) of that community may be. If we are to begin to envision and even to construct such a community or communities, we must begin with the realities we live, including our ideas and experiences of power.

POWER AS CONTROL

"Because I'm your mother, that's why."
"You'd better be careful; you could lose your job."
"It's just not natural."
"There is no salvation outside of the church."
You recognize them, examples of the familiar face of power as control. This understanding of power is so prevalent in our culture that it is difficult for many of us to image, to understand, and to embody power in any other form. Yet its very familiarity

can obscure its features. Ethnographic studies have taught us that a stranger will often identify aspects of a culture that the natives have never noticed. It is the stranger's questions that bring to the foreground what has only served as a backdrop to "ordinary life" and has been largely invisible. Likewise, experiences of cognitive dissonance call to our attention areas of the cultural map we navigate but that remained unseen as long as they were effective. The power with which we are most familiar in this culture is usually controlling, and often violent. Thus we need to be intentional about bringing it from the background to the forefront of our attention.

Power in and of itself is an ethically neutral concept. *Power* can be defined simply as "the ability to accomplish desired ends and social power as the ability of one individual or group to affect the behavior of another individual or group."[1] In this neutral sense, power can be understood as effectiveness, the ability to make one's choices operative in the world. Power as control, however, subordinates some through their domination by others, and for feminist scholars, the dynamics of domination constitute a fundamental category of injustice.[2]

I am choosing to use the term *power as control* rather than *power as domination* or *power over* to highlight the degree to which domination and manipulation work together in the dynamics of human relationships and institutions. Domination is often purposeful; we use a position of superior power, however defined and achieved, to manipulate another for our own ends. Thus the term *control* captures the aspects of both domination and manipulation; in the dynamics of power as control some persons are used by others as instruments to achieve the ends of the powerful.

Within the context of Christian theology, including its anthropology, power as control is inherently oppressive and unjust. Christians are committed to the conviction that all persons are created and equally beloved by God.[3] This conviction, in turn, grounds an obligation to include fundamental equality at least in a minimal sense as a feature of human community. That is to say that there is always a pull toward equality among persons based on their equal status before God, and inequality in Christian community requires justification. Often the principle of equality within Christian community is conceptualized as the agapic requirement of "equal regard."[4] However it may be expressed, it remains a resilient and persistent normative feature of Christian community. Thus a Christian ethic of community acknowledges the fundamentally equal value of all persons as a condition for justice.

Power as control assumes the superiority and the greater entitlement of one or some over another or others. By its very nature, power as control undermines and abrogates the commitment to fundamental, if minimal, equality to which all Christians are obligated. Therefore, power as control cannot function as the basis for a Christian ethic of community without deep and violent self-contradiction. Yet such power has been and is the most prevalent understanding and practice of power within Christian community.

Our knowledge and experience of power are only partly cognitive, only partly conscious. We experience it intuitively, emotionally, and physiologically. Hence I have chosen to present the heart of what we could term a "phenomenology of power as control" by way of illustration. We will look at two documents that embody in graphic ways the dynamics of power as control. The first is from the Middle Ages and may at first seem exotic. However, the relational dynamics are chillingly familiar. The second is from the New Testament. Its impact and import are both older and more recent than the fifteenth-century example, and it can act as an intellectual, historical, and experiential parenthesis.

MALLEUS MALEFICARUM: THE HAMMER OF WITCHES

The entire phenomenon of witchcraft as it was understood and practiced in the Middle Ages is fascinating to many persons today, Christian feminists among them.[5] From the fairy tale figures of our childhood to the novels and stagecraft of our more adult imaginations, the myths and reality of witchcraft seem to capture and hold the attention of generations of people.

Feminist historical reconstruction has taught us that witches were not the evil figures the patriarchal imagination usually sketched. They were sometimes socially powerful women but more often very weak ones who in any case were marginalized by their society and punished for their nonconformity. Christian feminists have become attuned to the power politics in the process of marginalizing groups of people, including the marginalization that results from the creation of heresy, and we recognize the misogyny at the heart of the heresy called "witchcraft."

Since the historical documentation that we have from the witch hunts and persecutions is a product of the persecutors and not of the women themselves, it is impossible to determine the degree to which we would or would not recognize the theological convictions of the "witches" as similar to our own. However, our recognition of the misogyny associated with the church's attitudes and behaviors toward witches alerts us to the possibility of a sympathetic interpretation of the lives and beliefs and practices of those whom the church labeled as "witch." We can at least imagine that some of their beliefs would be as comfortable to us, or more so, than those of their male persecutors who are our "fathers in the faith." For example, the feminist commitment to and experience of diversity includes our conviction that non-Christians can be spiritual healers. Furthermore, independent women who live apart from men in somewhat unconventional ways are not necessarily objects of fear and rejection but rather may be models and mentors from outside and within Christian feminism.

The historical phenomenon of witchcraft is fascinating not only for the degree to which it illuminates gender relations and church politics in various eras of the Middle Ages but also for the process of social construction that is discernible, and for what we can see of the dynamics of power as control.[6] Presumably people had been engaged in practices that were later labeled "witchcraft" before the category "witch" existed, and some of the practices associated with what became known as witchcraft, such as inexplicable healing and various psychic phenomena, continue in our day. Why, then, at certain points in history in certain cultures did Christian societies create the category "witch" and persecute persons who were identified as witches?

There is no complete and indubitable answer to that question.

What we do know is that certain conditions existed that can constitute a partial explanation for the appearance of witchcraft, and I will note four common assumptions that supported the phenomena of witchcraft in the Middle Ages.

First, witchcraft existed in societies in which sorcery or magic was believed to be real. In other words, one requirement for witchcraft is a belief that some persons are able to control what we might call spiritual and metaphysical "powers." Their ability to "effect their ends" extended to the manipulation of events that are normally outside of human control. Thus for those in power, controlling the controllers became both necessary and urgent.

Second, it was believed that personal misfortune had a causal explanation that included a moral component. Bad things did not happen to good people without a reason. If the reason were not the moral turpitude of the unfortunate one, it could easily be attributed to the malevolent will of another person. Morals and magic became intertwined in such a way that a person might defend his or her moral status by identifying the sorcerer responsible for the disease, crop failure, or sterile animal which would otherwise be explained on the basis of that person's own moral failure.

Third, it was widely assumed by both genders that males were superior to females—physically, morally, spiritually, and intellectually. Christians had to be careful to acknowledge the "goodness of women" on some level because they were an intentional part of God's creation. However, their goodness was accounted for by their instrumental value to the life of men. No genuine social equality was demanded by the God of Genesis 2 and the medieval church.

Finally, in the "witch-infested" areas of Europe, Christianity had obtained religious hegemony. The religious pluralism that Christianity had been forced to tolerate was submerged, if not eliminated, by Christendom. Christianity then had, and used, the power to suppress other belief systems—that is, the evil of witchcraft was a creation of Christianity. Again, the factors involved and the way those factors interrelated in certain societies at certain historical periods is a complicated story to reconstruct.[7] What we need to note is that in order for the heresy of witchcraft to exist, the institution of the Christian church also had to exist and to dominate and to define and to persecute the heresy.

Thus the four factors that are easily identified as key in the emergence of witchcraft as a heresy in the Middle Ages are a belief in magic, an insistence that misfortune had a specific cause traceable to human agency, the assumption that males were superior to females, and the theological and social hegemony of Christianity.

Like any social, cultural phenomenon that takes place in different geographical areas through several centuries, witchcraft was not a monolithic reality or even necessarily a consistent category of belief and practice. Thus to examine the dynamics of power as control in the identification and persecution of witches, I have chosen one document as a classic, though not comprehensive, treatise. It is called the *Malleus Maleficarum* or *The Hammer of Witches*. It was issued in 1486 under the authorship of the Dominicans Heinrich Kramer and Jacob Sprenger and with an introduction and imprimatur of Pope Innocent VIII. It is in essence a how-to manual for witch hunting. The full English translation is approximately 275 pages; its detail is both impressive and deeply unsettling.[8]

The document is divided into three parts, identified, as was usual in theological treatises of the time, as three questions. Part I describes how to identify a witch; Part II deals with methods of protecting against and undoing the effects of witchcraft; and Part III lays out the procedures for questioning and persecuting those thought to be witches. We do not share the world view that made the medieval understanding of witchcraft credible. Our very distance from that world view provides a good perspective from which to view the mechanics of power that were at work.

The witch hunts were classic examples of the exercise of power as control, and that control can be examined in four dimensions: *conceptual, behavioral, personal,* and *relational.*

A. Conceptual Control

First, and most fundamental, the churchmen possessed and exercised the power to interpret and thus to define reality. That is, they had and exercised control over how events were to be conceptualized and understood. A general belief in the practice of sorcery or magic did not necessarily translate into a fear of such practice. The activity of witches had to be defined in terms of an alliance with the devil in order to make it essentially malevolent and dangerous. By creating and controlling the metaphysical context of magic, the church provided the categories by which it had to be interpreted. In other words, alternative behavior, or behavior that may simply have had nothing to do with the church, became evil through the category of heresy. The power of the church that it identified with God was placed over against the power of witchcraft, which was identified with the devil. In order to protect the well-being and superior position of those who aligned themselves with the church, the church exercised its power to control persons' understanding of the "magical" events they witnessed.

By identifying witchcraft as an aspect of the presence of the devil in the world, and thus as a heresy, the church was able to create its nature not just as misguided, or as wrong, but as punishable. Furthermore, not only the practitioners of witchcraft but also all those who questioned the church's interpretation of events were subject to sanctions. In an appendix to the document, the faculty of theology of the University of Cologne added its approval of the contents and purpose of the *Malleus Maleficarum*. Reading between the lines, it is clear that approval was not unanimous among clergy, as this cumbersome statement illustrates:

> Whereas some who have the charge of souls and are preachers of the word of God, have been so bold as to assert and declare publicly in discourses from the pulpit, yea, in sermons to the people, that there are no witches, or that these wretches cannot in any way whatsoever molest or harm either mankind or beasts, and it has happened that as a result of such sermons, which are much to be reprobated and condemned, the power of the secular arm has been let and hindered in the punishment of such offenders, and this has proved to be a great source of encouragement to those who follow the horrid heresy of witchcraft and has very notably

increased and augmented their ranks, therefore the aforesaid Inquisitors, wishing with their whole hearts and strength to put a check unto such abominations and to counteract such dangers, have with much study, much research, and much labour, indited and composed a certain Treatise in which they have used their best endeavours on behalf of the integrity of the Catholic Faith to rebuke and rebut the ignorance of those who dare to preach so gross errors, and they have also been at great pains to set forth the lawful and proper way whereby these pestilent witches may be brought to trial, may be sentenced and condemned, according to the tenor of the aforesaid bull and the regulations of Canon Law.[9]

There was to be no open debate on the "reality of witchcraft." The authors of this document and their colleagues, who constituted the powerful majority, fundamentally exercised their power by defining, and controlling, the "truth."

B. Behavioral Control

The second arena in which power as control was exercised was that of behavior. The first category of control, that of defining reality, included defining to some extent what activities were and were not to count as witchcraft. However, the dividing line did not coincide with a definition of *magic* or *supernatural power,* for the church, too, claimed such power. So beyond defining what kinds of behavior constituted witchcraft, the church also was able to control the phenomenon by considering who benefited by the behavior, and on whose behalf it was done.[10]

The *Malleus Maleficarum* states clearly and consistently that the effects of witchcraft cannot be warded off or overcome by the use of witchcraft. Evil may not be employed even in the service of good. However, a whole section in Part II distinguishes between the "lawful" practices of exorcisms and the "unlawful spells" of witchcraft.[11] In addition, there are instructions for actions less dramatic than exorcisms, such as making the sign of the cross and sprinkling persons and objects with "holy salt" to protect Christians from the influence of witchcraft.[12] To a contemporary reader, the activities that are approved by the church are no less magical than those identified as witchcraft by the church and no more obviously benevolent. Thus the behavioral control exercised by the church manifested itself as approval of its own behavior and condemnation of that of others, even if the activities were remarkably similar. In other words, the power of the church to control witchcraft and witches included the power to control "good magic" and to punish "bad magic," the latter being defined as magic that the church did not control. The church created the heresy and provided the only available protection against it.

C. Personal Control

Who were the witches, and how did they understand themselves? There is information to give a partial answer to the first question, though there is much we do not know. Most people identified as witches were from the lower socioeconomic strata— that is, the powerless. At least four-fifths of all persons identified as witches were women. In fact, large sections of the first part of the *Malleus Maleficarum* are devoted to explaining *why* most witches are women; the pages of the document are sticky with misogyny.[13] Elsewhere the document describes the three primary methods by which devils use women who are already witches to "snare the innocent":[14] through "weariness," through "grievous losses in their temporary possessions," and "through the way of sadness and poverty" primarily caused from their rejection by lovers who they thought would be, or who were, husbands.[15] That is, those most likely to become witches were women who, by virtue of their gender, were already vulnerable and whose material conditions rendered them even more helpless and bereft of resources.

We can only speculate about how women who were identified as witches understood themselves. Even the documents that record their words at trials offer no reliable clues as to what they really thought of their situation. Did women who were weary, sad, impoverished and rejected turn to other women for solace even though it might have been dangerous to do so? Did the category of witchcraft itself offer some modicum of power to the utterly powerless so that the designation was attractive, even though it was identified with evil? Did the women, or some of them, internalize the definitions of their society such that their only categories of self-interpretation were those supplied by their persecutors?

Whatever the "witches" believed in their own hearts, the power of the church to control reality and to categorize behavior according to good and evil was the conceptual and behavioral framework with which these women had to operate, whether they believed it or not. Thus if their self-understanding was shaped by the categories of witchcraft, they could think of themselves as powerful and evil. If they rejected those categories, then they were assured of being misunderstood and unable to communicate their self-understanding because they were operating with assumptions that the church rejected. Furthermore, the church had the power to reinforce in very concrete ways its interpretation of reality. The witches remained powerless to impose their understanding on others. Their power was not the power to control in any meaningful and effective way, even with regard to their own lives.

As a haunting addendum to our speculations about the self-understanding of those accused of and even persecuted for witchcraft, let me note that the *Malleus Maleficarum* includes almost in passing the information that not all women who were witches were willing agents of the devil. The authors knew that to be the case because some women came to their trials bearing evidence of physical punishment, appearing with "blows and stripes" and "swollen faces." And some, after they confessed, tried to hang themselves.[16] Apparently the designation and the practice of witchcraft at times required physical force in addition to other forms of control, and some women had to be beaten into being witches.

D. Relational Control

It is highlighting the obvious to note that interpersonal relationships were controlled by those who defined reality, delineated approved behaviors, and designated the helpless as those against whom society needed protection. In addition to the blatant and unapologetic misogyny that infused the concept and persecution of witchcraft, the very methods recommended and used to identify and interrogate witches created suspicion among friends, neighbors, and family members and rendered the already helpless even more so.

The last part or question of the *Malleus Maleficarum* is devoted to detailed instructions about the identification and persecution of suspected witches. According to this document, anyone suspected of being a witch had to prove her innocence even if the only evidence against her was the testimony of someone known to be her enemy.[17] There were three conditions for imprisoning a suspected witch: her reputation, evidence of fact, and witnesses.[18] These may at first sound like rather rigid criteria. However, her reputation and "evidence of fact" could both be established by the testimony of one person who was known to have some personal vendetta against her. The witch was required to give testimony, but she was interrogated with torture until her testimony matched that of the "witnesses."[19] Furthermore, "evidence of fact" included her inability to cry in front of her judges, though witches were known to cry in private or in the presence of their jailers. Strength of character, or what we might call strong defense mechanisms, constituted damaging "facts" about her guilt.

In addition to torture, deceit was the preferred *modus operandi* for establishing guilt.[20] All sorts of persons, from jailers to old friends, were used by the persecutors to try to win the "witch's" trust and thereby to elicit a "confession." We can only imagine the personal devastation when in the context of such terrible danger even the support and confidence of friends and family proved illusory, deceptive, and finally condemnatory.

The powerful controlled the powerless by creating a climate of treacherous unpredictability in interpersonal relationships. In that climate, the powerless were labeled unpredictable and dangerous, and they were persecuted for the "safety" of the powerful. The real dangers of the society—rampant disease, unjust social and economic structures, the ravages of war, the vicissitudes of weather—which were outside the control of the church, were attributed to the behavior of those the church could control: persons labeled as witches.

29

Across the four dimensions of control—conceptual, behavioral, personal, relational—the assumptions of the powerful were powerfully reinforced. Magic was real and controllable; misfortune had an explanation; males were superior beings; Christianity held the "truth." The church was able to impose its will by controlling the world view of those within its walls and by punishing those who, for whatever reasons and in whatever way, found themselves outside. An examination of this somewhat "foreign" document exposes the anatomy of control that the church exercised in one time and place. It is now time to examine a more familiar document to see the same dynamics of power as control at work both in more ancient and in contemporary times.

EPHESIANS 5:21-33

We now move back in time to the first century of this era and forward to the present to view from another angle the face of power as control.

Written by a follower of Paul,[21] Ephesians is an energetic message to the early Pauline Christian communities, calling them to be what they claim they want to be: faithful followers and full embodiments of the risen Christ.[22] Ephesians is an elegant and eloquent record of the concerns of a church leader for young but strong Christian communities in Asia Minor toward the end of the first half century of Christian life. It is characterized by both congratulation and exhortation in a kind of exercise in moral cheerleading.

One of the most widely recognized theological departures in Ephesians from the genuine Pauline letters is its assumption of "realized eschatology." Ephesians is addressed to communities in which it is assumed that the Spirit of the risen Christ is fully present and in which Christian life may be fulfilled. Absent is the sense that there is more to come; neither the return of Christ in history nor a more spiritually interpreted parousia of the further unfolding of the will of God in time is part of the world view of the author of Ephesians.[23] The commendations and exhortations, then, reflect a kind of historical endstate, a vision of lives perfectly formed and blended together as a reflection of the body of Christ. Ephesians, in other words, does not suggest a transition stage on the way to something fuller, richer. Rather it illustrates this author's understanding of life in Christ as God means it to be.

Included in this understanding, this vision of communal life and interpersonal relationships, is a picture of power. That picture comes into focus at several places in the letter, and we will look at one of them: Ephesians 5:21-33, in which relationships between husbands and wives are structured.

> Be subject to one another out of reverence for Christ. Wives, be subject to your husbands as you are to the Lord. For the husband is the head of the wife just as Christ is the head of the church, the body of which he is the Savior. Just as the church is subject to Christ, so also wives ought to be, in everything, to their husbands. Husbands, love your wives, just as Christ loved the church and gave himself up for her, in order to make her holy by cleansing her with the washing of water by the word, so as to present the church to himself in splendor, without a spot or wrinkle or anything of the kind—yes, so that she may be holy and without blemish. In the same way, husbands should love their wives as they do their own bodies. He who loves his wife loves himself. For no one ever hates his own body, but he nourishes and tenderly cares for it, just as Christ does for the church, because we are members of his body. "For this reason a man will leave his father and mother and be joined to his wife, and the two will become one flesh." This is a great mystery, and I am applying it to Christ and the church. Each of you, however, should love his wife as himself, and a wife should respect her husband.

In our time, some commentaries and numerous articles have stressed the mutuality in this passage in order to suggest that the author is trying to mitigate the oppressive patriarchal subjugation of women within marriage. We are going to focus on the nature of power as it is reflected in the text and will return to the issue of mutuality in the last chapter.[24] Our text is part of the paraenetic section of Ephesians, a characteristic type of Pauline

31

injunction that urged Christians to conform in their behavior to what they already were through the grace of God. This subsection is introduced by the theme of imitation: "God in Christ has forgiven you. Therefore be imitators of God, as beloved children, and live in love, as Christ loved us and gave himself up for us, a fragrant offering and sacrifice to God" (Eph. 4:32*b*–5:2). Persons are to imitate God as a response to their forgiveness by God; that imitation is to be enacted as children imitate their parents. The behavior that "God's children" are to imitate is characterized by love exhibited in Jesus' sacrifice. With this analogy, an implicit equation is made between God's love for God's people and Christ's love for the church. The latter is not just one expression among many of the former but is its specification. God's love is embodied in the church.

The divine imprimatur upon the structure of the marital relationship is made explicit in our text when a husband's love for his wife is described as an imitation of Christ's love for the church. The imitation theme is used one more time: Christ's love imitates God's; a husband's love imitates Christ's; by implication, then, a husband's love imitates God's. This letter's structuring of the husband/wife relationship not only has a theological context, but it is understood to be an imitation of the relationship between God and God's people as well.[25]

What is the proper, Godlike ordering of the husband/wife relationship? It is a clear hierarchy, with the wife subject to the husband *for theological reasons*. As ordained by God and enacted in Christ's relationship with the church, the husband's love for the wife expresses itself as dominance. That is the shape of love in this text: one partner is dominant, the other submissive. Any other arrangement would not reflect the order of relationships ordained by God.

The author's advice to wives and husbands is not balanced. Only three verses are addressed to the wives; the content of the advice is the one command to be subject to their husbands. The other two verses contain the theological structure that supports the paraenesis. On the other hand, nine verses concern the husband's God-designated, Godlike relationship with his wife, and we learn much more about its content. First, the husband should love his wife as Christ loved the church. The effect of Christ's love on the church was to cleanse and purify it, making it holy and presumably, therefore, a fit spouse for Christ. The text then draws the parallel between the church as Christ's body and the wife as the husband's body. He is to love her as he loves his own body, just as Christ cares for his body, the church. Does the husband by his love somehow cleanse and purify the wife, making her a fit spouse for him, something that without him she would not otherwise be? The text does not say so explicitly, but the logic of the analogy would suggest that is the case. Thus, without her husband, her being is inadequate to her status as his spouse; it is his love that makes her worthy to be his wife, just as God's love makes the church worthy to be the bride of Christ.

Ephesians goes on to cite the creation story: man and wife will become one flesh. However, we already have learned whose flesh they both become—his. Thus as a result of being made worthy to be his wife, the woman loses her separate identity. Her choices are between being autonomous and unmarried or married and subsumed. And the theological rationale for this structure argues that such is God's will and has been so since the creation. It is, therefore, unalterable, even unquestionable. It is a given.

Power is exercised by God, by Christ, and by males. In this passage that power is called love. It is love that changes the nature of persons, into a church, into wives. Thus it manipulates the being of persons for God's ends and for men's ends. Furthermore, it is exercised in a pattern of dominance and submission, of God over persons, of Christ over the church, of husbands over wives. Husbands are subject to God and Christ the church, and what God and the church are ordering them to do is to be dominant over their wives. Thus both the elements of dominance and manipulation that characterize power as control are vibrantly present in this passage from Ephesians. The control is solidified by identifying it as the will of God from the beginning of time. It is baptized by interpreting Christ's relationship to the church as one of marriage.

There is evidence that the earliest Christian communities operated with a different understanding of power, what I call "power as life," and we will look at that in the next chapter. Here it is important to notice that by the time Ephesians was written and circulated, almost certainly early in the second century, power was understood and interpreted as control, and specifically and centrally included power of husbands over wives.[26]

What does mutuality mean in the context of a relationship structured according to a dominant/submissive pattern? Genuine reciprocity is not possible; interdependence becomes symbiosis. Exposing the structural relational skeleton assumed and advocated by Ephesians also exposes the impossibility of mutuality within the context of that structure.

CONTEMPORARY REVERBERATIONS

Very few people in our culture read or have even heard of the *Malleus Maleficarum,* though the phenomena of witches and witchcraft and witch hunting fascinate many. By contrast, the normative requirement for wives to be subject to their husbands is not only known but accepted by large segments of our culture, and the text we examined from Ephesians is familiar even to persons who could not identify its source. Ephesians 5 among other similar texts continues to exercise power in our culture and specifically within Christian congregations. Where and how does its face appear?

One of the most frequent locations is in support groups for battered women, especially those with Christian backgrounds and faith.[27] Women who are battered by their husbands, physically and/or psychologically, often believe that as awful as their husbands' behavior is, on some level the men have a right to treat their wives as they do. In a dominant/submissive relationship, especially one created and ordained by God, only one member of the relationship has any entitlement. In Christian marriage so understood, the wife relinquishes her separate identity and becomes an extension of her husband. Though many women would reject such a bald statement of the case, they actually behave as though they believe it when their husbands become abusive. They cannot articulate, never mind claim, any rights they as persons may have apart from the relationship with their husbands. Furthermore, many women deeply believe that they have a duty to try to modify their husbands' behavior by changing their own to comply with their husbands' desires and/or they have to stay to "take care of him" because if they left the men could not take care of themselves. The women actually have become extensions of their husbands' being.

The "battered women's movement," which has been part of this wave of feminism in this country, has generated much literature on the mechanics of spouse abuse. Among the range of cases, two facts emerge. First, the cases are diverse. Battering ignores all social and economic lines in this country. Second, regardless of the diversity of the persons involved, there is a startling similarity in the pattern of abusive behavior, and the fundamental mechanism of that pattern is control.[28] Whether the abuse takes the form of verbal belittling or has escalated to life-threatening physical violence, the abuse is in service of one person's control of another.

A common element among those who are victims of abuse is their sense that on some level they deserve it, that the behavior is appropriate.[29] Psychological reasons are often given—low self-esteem, learned helplessness, generalized feelings of guilt—and all of these play a role. I want to suggest as well that if one has entered a relationship in which all entitlements are relinquished and in which one person is understood as the dominant one with the power to control the other, then in some sense the abuse is appropriate, though not acceptable. That is, it follows logically from the structure of the relationship whoever the individuals may be who embody it.

Christian marriage as described by Ephesians 5 is so constituted that the male is dominant and the female is submissive. *That structure is inherently abusive* whether the abuse takes place or does not, and if it does not, its absence is in spite of and not because of the nature of the relationship. In other words, a marital relationship that is organized so that one partner is dominant and the other is submissive institutionalizes power as control. When the relationship is structured by and is a part of the church, then the institutionalization is understood to be, and is embodied as though it is, a reflection of the nature of the

God/human relationship and a faithful representation of God's desire for human community.

Could this be? Could power as control be what God wants at the foundation of Christian community, whether that community is understood as the relationship of marriage partners or is thought of as the church as a whole? Is God's face faithfully reflected in the witch hunters of the fifteenth century, in the author of Ephesians in the second century, or in spouse abusers in our own? Obviously I do not think so, and we will begin to examine an alternative picture in the next chapter.

CHAPTER TWO

THE OTHER FACE OF POWER:
POWER AS LIFE

The sights and sounds of the power of life are often muted in our world. They are not as shiny, not as shrill as those of power as control. Because of the prevalence of power as control in our world, we may not think of identifying the power of life as power. We may embrace it as joyful, delightful, even necessary, but not ultimately reliable in the face of all the violence in our world. Since the power of life is not controlling, it issues invitations, not ultimatums, and we need to become more attuned to hearing them, and perhaps more adept at responding. Again appealing to our knowledge that includes preverbal as well as verbal experience, here are some images of the power of life:

• A newborn child held by parents who are open and dedicated to the life they are creating, of which the child is a joyfully welcome part.
• The woman feeding her roses just after dawn, assisting and encouraging the growth of the garden that is the delight of the neighborhood.
• Handmade Christmas presents under a tree decorated with fun and silliness. Christmas carols and children's excited laughter and overexcited shouts and tears fill the air.
• Relief and gratitude when cancer goes into remission and the precious gift of life is felt all over again and prayers of thanksgiving are shared with family and friends.

• A classroom that feels safe and peaceful, and a teacher's honest, determined encouragement.
• The soul-tingling connection experienced between two people and with their God as they simultaneously and spontaneously break into applause after an especially glorious sunset.
• "I love you," said, and heard.

Power as life is power just as power as control is power. Power as life, too, is effective. Unlike power as control, it is generative, and it is not available for manipulation. It is something we join, cooperate with, not something we shape to our own ends. Rather, it helps to show us what our own ends are. It is never violent, though it may be felt as very forceful.

In this chapter we will look at two treatments of power as life. The first is Carter Heyward's phenomenology of power as erotic right relation in her book *Touching Our Strength: The Erotic as Power and the Love of God.* The second is Paul's exposition of the power of the cross in I Corinthians 1. Here, as in chapter 1, the emphasis is on presenting the characteristic features of this type of power rather than offering sustained, detailed argument since our understanding and experiences of power are precognitive as well as conceptual. If we are to rethink power, we must begin to refeel it as well, and for the latter, our imaginations are as important as our rational analysis.[1]

Many contemporary feminists, both Christians and non-Christians, have criticized power as it is conceptualized and embodied in patriarchal contexts and have offered an alternative conception. Audre Lorde's essay "Uses of the Erotic: The Erotic of Power" was one of the first. This essay has been deeply influential, and many feminists, including Carter Heyward, have adopted and adapted her insights.[2] I have chosen Heyward's treatment of what I am calling "power as life" for two reasons. First, she is working within the context of *Christian* feminism, however marginal her work may seem to the church,[3] and her characterization of erotic power is an elegant rendering of insights shared by other Christian feminists. Second, she offers a radical critique of the cross as a symbol for relational power, and again her critique is representative of objections voiced by other feminist scholars.[4] Thus part of my argument for the reclamation of the cross as an important symbol for Christian feminist communal ethics will be constituted by the resonances I will indicate between Heyward's conception of eroticism and Paul's understanding of the cross as symbols of the power of God. Furthermore, since Heyward's objections to the cross as a symbol for Christian feminist ethics are, at least in outline, representative of the objections of other feminist thinkers, my conversation with her thought addresses the general concerns of the Christian feminist community.

I have chosen Paul as an early messenger of the power of the cross as the power of life first because his letters offer us the clearest picture of a group of people struggling to understand and embody a "new world," a world shaped by a power that seemed odd and surprising and that called forth new ways of being together in community. Second, Paul's letters, especially I Corinthians 1, offer a sustained if not a systematic discussion of the cross and its implications for Christians' understanding and embodiment of power.[5]

As noted above, my argument against Heyward's critique of the cross as a symbol for the power of life will be crafted in a later chapter. Now I will simply present my understanding of Heyward's characterization and my interpretation of Paul's characterization side by side so that the similarities can emerge on their own.

THE EROTIC AS POWER AND THE LOVE OF GOD

Carter Heyward's writing is intentionally evocative. She implicitly and explicitly rejects a purely cognitive discussion and bases her analyses on intuition and experience as well as on cognition and thus appeals to both in her readers. Her method and her message are in harmony.[6]

Heyward is a Christian theologian, and her understanding of God is integral to her understanding of power. She speaks of the nature of God and God's power in many ways; this one is representative:

God is our relational power. God is born in this relational power. God is becoming our power insofar as we are giving birth to this sacred Spirit in the quality of our lives in relation, the authenticity of our mutuality, the strength of our relational matrix.

It is a paradox: God is becoming our relational matrix insofar as we are the womb in which God is being born. This may be easier to comprehend if we substitute the word "love" for "God." Love is becoming our relational matrix if we are the womb in which love is being born. Love is becoming our home if we are lovers. God is becoming our power in relation to the extent that we are coming into our power as lovers of one another.[7]

As this long quotation expresses, God is a relational concept for Heyward. God is *not* a remote figure, independent of persons, unaffected by human life and choices. We are at home in God, and God is at home in us. God is our relational power.

God is a relational power, which can be born in us, realized in our lives, but not manipulated to our ends, or that power becomes something else besides God. From this fundamentally relational base, Heyward suggests a series of equivalences that flesh out the nature of the relational power that God is.

God is the power of right relationship, which is mutuality expressed as justice, and right relationship constitutes justice.[8] Again, Heyward is not developing a systematic theological ethic; these equivalences are not definitional but rather represent different aspects of the same power. Thus the power of relationship that is God is right relationship, which is just and mutual.[9]

Mutuality can be a slippery concept, in Heyward's work and elsewhere. Without attempting a full development of the concept, let me simply note that for Heyward mutuality can best be paraphrased as interdependence. It is the recognition and experience of our need for one another and our effectiveness in benefiting one another. It is our experience of loving and being loved.

We can gain some clarity and detail regarding Heyward's use of the concept of mutuality by turning to another feminist Christian ethicist, Beverly Harrison. She speaks of mutuality as loving one another into being.

It is within the power of human love to build up dignity and self-respect in each other or to tear each other down. We are better at the latter than the former. However, literally through acts of love directed to us, we become self-respecting and other-regarding persons, and we cannot be one without the other. If we lack self-respect we also become the sorts of people who can neither see nor hear each other.[10]

A claim about the centrality of mutuality reflects the recognition of our interdependence even for our own sense of self. There is a free-verse poem that hangs in many pediatricians' offices that begins, "Children learn what they live." Persons are formed by the nature of the relationships of which they are a part, and the process does not end at some point in adulthood. We literally have the power to enhance or diminish one another. That fact reflects our mutuality. And mutuality that is just is always for the purpose of enhancing, not diminishing.

For Heyward, then, God is the power that humans can exercise to love one another into being, the power of right relationship, which is mutuality expressed as justice. It is both a capacity to love and the exercise of that capacity, ours to participate in but never control. It requires its exercise in our lives to become effective; we require it to love and acknowledge love from another.

Heyward insists that we need to notice that this power *is* power. She writes, "We may believe that the mutuality we experience in relation to some others is *good,* but we have not learned to trust it as *powerful*: the fulcrum of our capacity to survive and to affect the world around us."[11]

Mutuality, our capacity to enhance others and be enhanced by them, seems a soft thing, nice but not necessary, certainly not necessary for survival. Compared to the power that is violent, the power to love may seem weak or even impotent.

On the contrary, Heyward claims that what I am calling the power of life is the foundation of a revolution of understanding and behaving that must take place if we are to survive as a people and a planet.[12] In order to escape the destructive patterns of domination and submission that have contaminated us all, we must move in the direction of just mutuality. And it is precisely mutuality justly lived that can overcome the old destructive patterns, not by violently obliterating them but by gently, slowly replacing them with the power to love and be loved. As Heyward says:

> It is vital, morally and spiritually, that we realize that we all participate in these fundamentally flawed relational dynamics of domination and submission. We can't escape them entirely without leaving the world. But we can help create a better way. To do so we need one another's friendship and solidarity. We must be patient, persevering, and tender with one another and ourselves. It will take years, decades, a long time, to learn, with one another, that our power to love is stronger than the fear that festers in our alienation.[13]

According to Heyward, our access to this relational power for just mutuality is our sensuality, our eroticism. Following Lorde, by "the erotic" Heyward does not mean simply genital sexuality. She means our ability, and our embodied need, to touch one another and to be touched by one another.

Touching is first of all physical. It is also spiritual. Our ordinary language is full of the connection between the two. We say that something is "touching" if it evokes a connection with someone or something else. We say that "you touched me deeply" if something you said or did seems to reach into the heart of our being.

Lorde, Heyward, and other feminists use the term *eroticism* to appeal to our experience of the multi-faceted reality that human touching encompasses. In the deeply dualistic thought patterns that contaminate all Western thinking, even to some degree the thought of those who consciously reject it, it is difficult to conceptualize with any clarity those human experiences that do "touch" all aspects of the person. Thus the physical/emotional/spiritual connections in these experiences remain dim, misty, perhaps not powerful. Yet it is precisely the power of those connections, which happen "to" people only "with" people, that is the power of life and renewal that constitutes the foundation of the moral and political revolution in our patterns of living together that Heyward envisions.

Eroticism may seem like a shocking, inappropriate term to use to evoke the reality and power of God. It is shocking precisely because of the dualistic thinking that wants to keep God's touch "spiritual" and sexuality genital. It is shocking in the context of a Protestant spiritual sensibility that confuses the Word with words, and that wants to confine God's access to our intellects. It is shocking in the context of Christian ethics that begin and end with rules, because our experience of eroticism is that it dances around and through many rules. Eroticism is a shocking container for the Spirit of God if our need is control.

Eroticism is a marvelous description of our need to reach out and touch one another and be touched. It captures the spontaneity and unpredictability of where and how we are touched, and how we touch others. A personal observation is in order here: One of the most remarkable experiences for me when I began my ministry was learning how poorly I was able to predict which sermons would and would not "touch" people. There is a power of transmission, an agency of tenderness and confrontation, that does not originate with me, that is not in my control, but for which I am the catalyst. It is a remarkable, and powerful, partnership. And it is erotic. Nothing is left untouched.

Eroticism as a term for the power of life is a marvelous reminder of the holistic nature of personal experience. It also reminds us of the holistic nature of God. It leaves God out of our control, and leaves us with the responsibility to live into the power of God, which is the power to enhance one another.

Touching may heal, or it may harm; it may enhance, or it may diminish. Touching may kill as well as call forth life. Heyward's use of the term *eroticism* forestalls the possibility that we would confuse the power of God with the power to harm and kill. Eroticism invites the touch of another, opens us, stretches us toward the arms of another. Touching that harms us closes us up, shrinks us inward. Eroticism urges us to run toward another; touching that harms makes us want to run away. And we know, in the very fiber of our being, the difference between the two. If touching has hurt us too badly, it may take a long time for us even to take the risk of feeling the power of God, but it is only in being touched by the power of God, offered patiently, tenderly, over and over, that the hurt will be healed and we can grow again. The power of life is stronger, finally, than the power that harms or kills.

Heyward, then, identifies, sketches, evokes our experience of the power of God as relational and incarnate in human lives. Her use of the term *erotic* to characterize that power is suggestive of a kind of holistic "YES" that we say to the beloved, ourselves, all creation as we love one another, touch one another into life. And that life-giving, love-giving power *is power.* It is a revolutionary force that rejects our attempts to divide and control, whether we are attempting to divide and control God, the cosmos, other people, or aspects of human life. It heals and it brings forth more life whenever it is embodied. It is not contained but spills over. We, God, the power of life are deeply relational, and deeply powerful.

Carter Heyward discusses eroticism, the power of life, and the relational nature of God from a radically feminist position. Her theological ethics peels away layers of patriarchal barnacles to expose what she sees as the core of the relationship between God and humans and some central features of each. Her work is revolutionary and Christian; her analysis and use of the concept of eroticism functions within a radically feminist Christian framework. In order to be clearer about eroticism as it is used here, let us briefly contrast it with the concept of *jouissance* as it functions in the writings of the French feminist Julia Kristeva. This contrast will do two things: It will bring into sharper focus the concept of the power of the cross as eroticism, and it will identify from a different perspective some of the contours of our understanding and practice of power that the Christian dimension introduces.

JOUISSANCE: A CONTRAST

Julia Kristeva is one of the most creative and important contributors to both feminist and postmodernist thought. Her critique and development of Freudian psychoanalytic theory expand its frontiers; her analysis of gender and language and the ways these function, and do not function, in the formation of the human being is bold, complex, and provocative. I certainly do not intend a full discussion of her theories; nor do I pretend to offer even a digest of all of her thought. I want only to say enough about her general approach to be able to discuss her use of the concept of *jouissance* and to offer it as a helpful contrast to the eroticism that is so important to the thought of Carter Heyward and other American feminists and to the power of the cross as I have been describing it.

There are many intellectual streams feeding Kristeva's thought, including Russian structuralism and Marxism.[14] However, for our purposes, her thought can be described as an intriguing blend of poststructuralist linguistic theory and psychoanalysis with peculiar feminist twists.[15] Two fundamental concepts for Kristeva are "the symbolic" and "the semiotic." The symbolic is the interpreted world, the "Word of the Father," the realms of culture, logic, science, "formal" religion. Her description and use of the symbolic have strong resonances in American feminist scholars' depiction of patriarchal epistemology and morality.[16] Though she does not speak in these terms, it is the realm of power as control where control of primitive, prerational drives and impulses is precisely the point. Developmentally, the symbolic emerges in relationship to the father and in separation from the mother in a rather classically Freudian depiction. It both represents and enacts order, structure, conformity, all that Freud understood by "civilization."[17] The Symbolic, as Kristeva uses the concept, functions as a kind of psychoanalytic LOGOS, a paternal ordering principle present in, even marking, the beginning of consciousness and identity.

In Kristeva's thought, the symbolic is contrasted with the semiotic. The semiotic is the maternal element, the prelinguistic, connected, embodied experience of the infant with the mother. It is primitive, instinctual, erotic in a prereflective sense. The semiotic is submerged by the symbolic, but it is never eliminated, at least not in the experience of females. In Kristeva's analysis, the semiotic is an ongoing part of female reality since we are never able fully to identify with the father, and therefore not with the symbolic, though we participate in it.[18] Furthermore, the semiotic is never entirely controlled by the symbolic; it has a subversive or transgressive quality, which presumably renders it at least potentially revolutionary.[19] However, the moment we would begin to organize or even to conceptualize the semiotic, it becomes part of the symbolic and thus loses its transgressive, potentially revolutionary character. Thus it exists at the edges, marking the boundaries of the rational and orderly and not in itself subject or amenable to either.

It is within the realm of the semiotic that Kristeva locates and discusses *jouissance*. The French word *jouissance* can be translated "joy," but as Kristeva and other French feminist philosophers use the term, it is earthier than the English term *joy*. In Kristeva's work it can also be translated "female orgasm." As such it is both intense and diffuse. She also speaks of it in connection with pregnancy. It is more the rich, alive, erotic female experience outside of the symbolic than it is about being pregnant and giving birth, which no male language, no "Word of the Father" can ever quite capture. It is the profoundly arousing experience of nursing an infant that medical descriptions of nursing, even those produced by La Leche League, never quite capture and which we women can only indicate and perhaps recognize when we ourselves have the experience. *Jouissance* is the mire and mess of embodied life, sticky and often smelly and above all grounded and therefore at least partly inaccessible to abstractions. It is intensely alive, full—joy.

Even within the framework of her psychoanalytic and poststructural linguistic categories, there is clearly some overlap between Kristeva's concept of *jouissance* and Heyward's and other American feminists' use of "the erotic." Both are resistant to and destroyed by control. Both are identified and described primarily in terms of female experience. Both are intensely embodied concepts and therefore not fully accessible to the abstraction of language—the symbolic in Kristeva's terminology. Both allude to elements of playfulness, of joy, of the sheer delight of being.

The contrast, however, is as instructive as the similarities. *Jouis-*

sance as Kristeva uses the term is essentially chaotic. Consistent with her Freudian orientation, Kristeva posits as opposites the symbolic of "the father" and the semiotic of "the mother" and goes on to identify them with the male and female genders. Thus any imposition or introduction of order, conceptualization, or analysis destroys *jouissance*. Furthermore, it seems to be an experience, or better, quality of experience, available only to females, since in order for males to develop as males they must identify with the father and separate, and distance themselves from, the mother. *Jouissance,* then, is a fundamentally parasitic concept, dependent for its existence on the presence of the symbolic.[20] In a strangely Hegelian-sounding dialectic, Kristeva claims that in this world, *jouissance* is most fully expressed as pregnancy and madness. Psychosis is the "language" of *jouissance.*

In contrast to *jouissance,* the erotic as the power of life embraces order, though not control.[21] It precedes but does not preclude conceptualization. We can describe the process of life, though never fully, of course. Our descriptions, if they are careful, do not destroy the erotic but may even serve to enhance it if the conversation renders the erotic more familiar and more trustworthy. The erotic is not an essentially parasitic category but a fundamentally creative one. It is embodied but not necessarily and all the time bodily; Audre Lorde speaks of the eroticism of writing a poem as well as of making love.[22]

More radically, *jouissance* begins with a fundamental split, a basic division, between males and females. Our very gendered development depends on separation from the mother. Males can accomplish that more completely than females. Because the female's separation from the mother is never complete, there are whole areas of her experience that are not subsumed by male experience and language. However, it is also unavailable to male experience and language—that is, to the symbolic, public, intelligible realm. It is a kind of primitive private world whose only public language is that of psychosis.

Eroticism, as I have been using the concept, does not depend on a fundamental, ontological, or even existential split between the genders. We may acknowledge the historical fact that males and females are socialized differently in our culture, and that given the different socialization, females tend to be more open to the power of the erotic and have certainly been more articulate about it. The freedom and play of eroticism, power experienced not as control but as life, may be more familiar to females in our culture than to males. However, that is not an essentialist claim but a historical and social one that is open to change. Eroticism is available to both males and females.

Jouissance is predicated upon a fundamental division between the genders. The source of the erotic is a fundamental unity: the power and connection of and with God. From a Christian perspective, the unity is prior to whatever divisions we may find among humans.[23] Furthermore, the claim that gender is the fundamental division of humanity may itself reflect a white, middle-income construction of reality. [24] It is certainly one human determinate, but depending on one's social location, it may not be the central one. If gender is not construed as *the* basic human category, *jouissance* itself becomes less intelligible and perhaps even somewhat experientially remote. Finally, *jouissance* depends on the ongoing power of primal connections to mother and father. Eroticism assumes a god beyond mother and father, and it does not require either a dependent child or an adult that has left the child behind. With the power of the cross, maturity is measured by responsiveness and concern for others as well as oneself, not by separation from anyone.

With this contrast in mind, let us consider Paul's vision of the power of the cross.

THE CROSS AS THE POWER OF GOD

Paul may seem like an odd match with Carter Heyward, and in many ways, of course, he is. Almost two millennia and untold cultural differences separate the two, and they operate with different agendas and in some central respects different theological contexts. However, they are engaged in a similar enterprise: the task of reshaping Christian community around an understanding of power as the power of life. For Heyward, that life is expressed as erotic mutuality. For Paul, it is understood as new life and resurrection. For both, power is relational, incarnational, and generative of new forms of human connection and community.

Paul's project was that of forming Christian communities in accordance with his understanding of the Christ event.[25] The Christ event included, but of course was not limited to, an understanding of power as a life-giving force stronger than violence and death imposed and supported by religious and political "powers." This new understanding of power made possible a new perception, a new way of understanding the world, of assigning values, of relating one to another. Thus it made possible a new vision and to some extent a new embodiment of community.

We can talk of Paul's community forming and community building as a process of resocializing persons into a new way of life.[26] Resocialization is familiar to us all; it is the process of adapting to a new social environment. It may be minor or extensive, depending on the degree to which old patterns of perceiving and relating need to be modified. It may involve anything from learning the routines in a new office setting, both those spoken and unspoken, to adapting to major life changes that take place as a result of a move to another culture or a religious conversion. Obviously change is never total, and resocialization does not take place *ex nihilo*. It is, rather, a matter of rearranging old patterns according to a new center, adding some things, eliminating others, in response to new settings and new requirements. Paul's letters reflect this process of resocialization, the formation of communities that included a dramatically new understanding of the power of God.

In I Corinthians 1 Paul describes this new understanding of power:

> For the message about the cross is foolishness to those who are perishing, but to us who are being saved it is the power of God. For it is written,
> > "I will destroy the wisdom of the wise,
> > > and the discernment of the
> > > discerning I will thwart."
> Where is the one who is wise? Where is the scribe? Where is the debater of this age? Has not God made foolish the wisdom of the

world? For since, in the wisdom of God, the world did not know God through wisdom, God decided, through the foolishness of our proclamation, to save those who believe. For Jews demand signs and Greeks desire wisdom, but we proclaim Christ crucified, a stumbling block to Jews and foolishness to Gentiles, but to those who are the called, both Jews and Greeks, Christ the power of God and the wisdom of God. For God's foolishness is wiser than human wisdom, and God's weakness is stronger than human strength. (I Cor. 1:18-25)

Some persons in the Corinthian community were boasting of their wisdom, setting themselves above others in the community, and threatening schisms based on what sounded like competing loyalties to different evangelists.[27] Paul posits the reversal of wisdom and foolishness, power and weakness, based on the action of God in the cross of Jesus Christ.[28] Those who boast of their greater wisdom do so in accordance with old understandings of wisdom. "Christ crucified" becomes the new standard for wisdom, a standard that flies in the face of the interpretive and experiential categories of both Jews and Greeks (or Gentiles; Paul uses the terms interchangeably) and renders the old categories "foolish." And "Christ crucified" becomes the new standard for power.

Just as those who have been deemed wise according to the old standards are now deemed foolish, so also are the standards for interpreting and exercising power overturned by "Christ crucified." The old standards of power are familiar to us; the might of the Roman Empire was marshaled in service of religious control and it manifested violence and intimidated persons through threats of more violence. God's power did not directly confront those forces with more force, though there are many places in the Bible where that is how God's power is depicted.[29] God's power as shown forth in "Christ crucified" is the reversal of power as violent control. It is the power to bring life, even in the face of the worst, most destructive power that can be brought to bear.

Paul writes that "God's weakness is stronger than human strength" (I Cor. 1:25b). It is, of course, ironic for Paul to characterize God as weak. Rather, Paul appeals to a new understanding of power that is in contrast with the old and that is characteristic of God, shown forth in the cross and resurrection of Jesus Christ. By the old standards, with the old "wisdom," this power seems like weakness. What the cross and resurrection teach is that this power, which looked like weakness, is really the greatest power of all, the power of God.

The language of contrast that Paul uses in I Corinthians 1 could suggest that the power of the world and the power of God exist in some sort of dialectic tension. They could be interpreted as being the mirror image of each other, negative reflections, so that if a person had an understanding of one, that person could also perceive and understand the other. This interpretation is precluded by the element of surprise, even of shock, that Paul includes in his description of the power of God. It is precisely the fact that we could not predict the nature of the power of God based on the standards of the world that constitutes the sharp edge of rebuke in this passage for those who would claim that they could grasp the power of the cross with worldly wisdom. The first-century Christians, and we, are not equipped by common understandings and expressions of power as control to perceive as power the noncoercive, nonmanipulative, nondominating power for which the cross is the central symbol in Paul's writing. In fact, as we look for signs of power based on an understanding of power as control, we will be fooled into thinking that noncontrolling signs of life are weak, vulnerable to coercion, manipulation, domination, even crucifixion.

For Paul, the lesson of the cross is that even the most violent efforts to manipulate life, to control the power of God, are finally overcome by that very power that by worldly standards looks like weakness. (We will consider this point in detail in chapter 4.) It is important to realize the degree to which we still operate with an understanding, and practices, of power as control and that we still struggle to identify and experience "power as life." We cannot grasp the latter on the basis of our knowledge of the former; mirror reading does not work. We must perceive and intend a reality altogether different from the old understanding, as different as the cross is from the soldier's sword.

With the power of the cross at the center of understanding and practice, human life in relationship to God looks and feels different in many important respects, and life is, in many important respects, new. Paul has two conceptions of the new life in Christ: "resurrection from the dead and new life now lived in Christian community."[30] According to Paul's discussion in I Corinthians 15, resurrection from the dead is important because it reveals and confirms that God's power is more powerful than death,[31] but by far the preponderance of his attention is to the possibilities for life now in Christian community formed and shaped by the new understanding of power that the life, death, and resurrection of Jesus Christ make possible.

Christian community rightly formed is the ongoing incarnation of the power of God; Paul even refers to the community as the body of Christ. It is the place where the power of God lives and is realized in the world, in both the noetic and the ontological senses of the word *realized*. Thus though Paul never draws this conclusion explicitly, what is at stake in his attempts to "build up" communities based on "Christ crucified" is the very efficacy of the power of God in the world. The logic of Paul's theology, if not his actual claims, depicts the relationship between God and Christian community as one of partnership and mutuality. God is encountered and experienced in community in ways that are simply not possible otherwise. And the community shows forth the presence of God in the world in a radically unique way as it embodies the reality of the power of the cross.[32] It is odd if not startling to argue that the apostle of grace was writing of a partnership between God and humanity. If one continues to insist on a conception of God as a controller—if, in other words, the power of God is not interpreted through the cross but rather by "worldly" standards—the relationship between God and persons is one of control, as large parts of the Christian tradition have interpreted it. If, however, we apply Paul's radical interpretation of the power of the cross to our understanding of the nature of God, the relationship between God and persons is quite different from that of our absolute dependence on God. Paul's consistent claims about the power of God being lived out in Christian community, when coupled with his interpretation of the power of the cross, lead to a construal of the relationship between God and humanity that has greater similarities to Carter Heyward than to Luther or Calvin.

The power of God that was shown forth in the cross is made manifest in Christian community. What is that power in community? Here Paul is explicit: It is the power to "build one another up," to enhance the well-being of others based on their concrete reality. The presence of the risen Christ in community makes possible not only a rich relationship with God but also a love that involves commitment to the well-being of the other. It provides the insight and the motivation to treat others with respect and to be responsive to their needs.

Paul does not recommend self-sacrifice as the model for human behavior, though the needs of the other are to count as much as one's own needs. Rather, time and time again in his letters he exhorts Christians to understand first that the power of God is available to them as they change from a way of life that was concerned with being better than others to a way of life that was concerned with loving others. Second, he insisted that the well-being of each Christian depends on the well-being of the whole community, for it is in the attitudes and behavior of the community that the power of God is manifest. The incarnation of God in the world is deeply relational, and Paul's relational theology is deeply incarnational.

The power of the cross, then, functions as a kind of organizing principle for Christian community. It is not power that dominates or manipulates, though it may call persons to task for harming others (and in this radically communal vision, what harms one harms all). It is power that enables loving in concrete ways, taking account of the actual needs of the other and the actual needs of oneself. It is a power that values unity, harmony, and fairness more than impressive behavior by some individuals with the effect of intimidating others.

In the world in which Paul lived and worked, as in ours, it must have been difficult to sustain one's focus on the insight that the power of the cross, the power to generate life even in the face of the most violent destruction, is genuine power. It must have been difficult to continue to learn and live new ways of interacting so that one knew at deeper and deeper levels that one's own well-being depended on that of others. It must have been difficult to trust, really trust, that in spite of the continuing reality of violence and domination and manipulation in the world, real power, the power that ultimately gives life, does not resort to such tactics or it destroys itself as well as those around it.

Paul's constant encouragement to the communities he founded and those to whom he wrote was in part his attempt to help them retain or regain that focus. The coming together of persons in this great communal experiment was apparently a powerful experience for many, and he reminded them of that experience so that they would not begin to think that the power of life was impotent in the face of the power of death.

CONCLUSION

At first glance it would seem that the rich, sensual, fluid, relational concept of eroticism as discussed by Carter Heyward would stand in utter contrast to the stark, bleak, desolate reality of the cross of Jesus Christ. The one is a fully embodied celebratory experience of life. The other is thought of as a symbol of death.

However we interpret the relationship between them, both stand as challenges to and denials of the ultimacy of power as control, though they do not condemn us to the chaos of *jouissance*. Furthermore, to interpret the cross as a symbol of death is to reject Paul's insight and argument that the cross is a symbol of life, of the final impotence of violence in the face of death. Just as the cross appears to symbolize impotence but is in fact our best hermeneutic of power, so also it appears to mean death; but in fact it signals new life that we could not otherwise imagine. Like the spontaneity and playfulness of eroticism, which cannot be controlled without being lost, the cross eludes our attempts to tame it through manipulation and domination, either conceptual or institutional. Both eroticism and the cross beckon us to new and unpredictable life that requires human embodiment to be fully realized in the world.

CHAPTER THREE

FOUR DIMENSIONS OF POWER

POWER AS CONTROL—POWER AS LIFE

The phenomenon, the experience, and the images of power as control are familiar, internalized, convincing. We recognize the dynamics of the witch hunts as those in control track down and punish the deviance they themselves define. We see those dynamics at work in an exemplary way in the spouse abuse that knows no social boundaries in our society. We hear them in the words that our churches call Holy Scripture. We practice them in our daily lives, practice that is "natural" for those with racial, sexual, social, and economic privilege.

Power as life is no less prevalent, but we are often untrained to recognize it and therefore fail to designate it as power. Human birth itself, of course, even in the medicalized middle-income experience, is seen and celebrated as an expression of and participation in power. We still speak unashamedly of "the miracle of birth" as the complexities of the known mechanics of conception and gestation in the generation of another human being are as amazing as they are explainable. Apart from this paradigmatic expression of power as life, we are aware, or can be made aware, of life-giving, life-sustaining power in the sensual, erotic connectedness of persons with one another and with the world around us. Furthermore, some strands in the Christian tradition affirm the power of life even over death, the power of our connectedness even through the experience of what seems to be the ultimate separation.[1] Paul's understanding of the power of the cross in I Corinthians is an example of that affirmation.

With the evocation of our experiences of power as control and power as life presented by the previous chapters before us now and as a prelude to the discussion of the power of the cross in the next chapter, I want to deepen and expand our sensibilities by looking at the two forms of power in four dimensions: *interpersonal, institutional, cultural,* and *theological.* I intend this description to function as a conceptual road map only, not as a definitive analysis of what is after all a dynamic reality.[2] I will speak of the four dimensions as ever widening and increasingly distant contexts. They are not, however, helpfully imaged as concentric circles; first, they are dynamic phenomena, and second, unlike concentric circles, they touch each other at various and varying points. The experience of power at the interpersonal level will affect not only the expression but also the interpretation of power in the other three dimensions; interpersonal power itself is understood and enacted within institutional, cultural, and theological contexts that shape us all.

The conceptual road map is necessary because our lives do move in these dimensions, and any revisioning and reconfiguration of human community must take account of and address all of them. White, middle-income feminists, for example, experience the recurring frustration of attempting to reconstitute human community on the interpersonal and even institutional level, only to find that cultural privilege draws us back into the same patterns of thinking, feeling, and behaving that we struggle so to leave behind. Or we move more or less successfully into another culture and help to shape it, only to find that on the interpersonal level our lives are characterized more by control than by life-giving power. Not only the project of thinking an ethic of community but more important the project of attempting to live one requires that we attend to several dimensions of power and the ways they interact.

POWER AS INTERPERSONAL

Feminists have been concerned with, attentive to, and prolific with regard to issues of interpersonal power since the beginning of this wave of feminism. It is the case that persons who are disenfranchised in the wider culture may be able to exercise only minute amounts of personal power and then only in subversive ways.[3] It has been part of the genius of feminist scholarship to analyze and document the impossibility of separating in any clear or meaningful way issues of interpersonal power and power that can be exercised in broader arenas. In this discussion I will distinguish, but not separate, the different levels of power.

How do the two forms of power that we have been discussing manifest themselves in the interpersonal sphere? As we have already seen, power as control manifests itself as abuse.[4] One person or group uses another person or group for their own ends, thereby abusing the nature of each group as human. Control of persons is never complete; the threat, if not the reality, of losing control is always present. The fundamental insecurity that is an intrinsic feature of control manifests itself as the need to reinforce control, to shore up resources and patterns that exert control. However, as the level of control escalates, so does the level of insecurity. When the threat or the perceived threat is sufficient, violence results.

It is important to note that control of one person or group of persons by another is itself abusive and is the mechanism of abuse. Violence is a tool of control, not the fundamental dynamic. We see the dramatic effects of interpersonal control that has become violent in the swollen eyes and bruised bodies of its victims, but invisible violence also bruises and leaves scars on the human spirit. The level of insecurity and desperation of the one who holds power over another can be read off in the degree of violence that accompanies the control. Power as control is itself damaging.

Less familiar, perhaps, but no less dramatic are the manifestations of power as life. I want to introduce now a concept that I have intentionally avoided to this point because it can be so terribly misleading: the power of life as love. I have avoided using the

57

term for a number of reasons. First, it evokes a panoply of images and concepts; the word *love* is used to cover a large and often incongruent set of human emotions and experiences. Second, in our culture at least, the word *love* is commonly taken to mean a feeling, and though an affective element is part of the phenomenon of love, it is far from the entire content.

The reality of love is too powerful and too valuable to abandon, however misleading the term may be in certain contexts; within a Christian ethic, it is finally indispensable. Love as I am using it is synonymous with power as life. Love is both a posture and a set of practices that call forth and sustain life, both physical and spiritual. It is a posture of fundamental benevolence, an attitude that favors the well-being of the other. It is an attentive posture, inclined toward another, sensitive to the concrete reality that the other is.[5] Love is also a set of practices that are responsive to and responsible for the well-being of another and of others.[6] Since the concrete shape of acts of love is determined in part by the nature and needs of the lovers, it cannot necessarily be programmed in advance. Spontaneity and ritual neither contradict nor diminish each other as they characterize the practices of love.

Broken lives and tattered spirits are the results of the ongoing experience of power as control and abuse. Rich lives and strong healthy spirits are the creations of love. In 1980, Beverly Harrison wrote, "We do not yet have a moral theology that teaches us the aweful, awe-some truth that we have the power through acts of love or lovelessness literally to create one another."[7] Since 1980, Harrison herself and other feminist writers have worked hard on developing a moral theology that highlights the relationality of persons and the formative impact that the relational web in which we exist has on our very identities. Furthermore, that impact is relevant not only for who loves us and how but also for whom and how we love others.

We either love one another into being or we fail to do so. Physical birth is only the beginning of the birthing process in which we humans engage. The power of life as love calls forth a depth and breadth of emotional, intellectual, and spiritual capacities— for joy, for nurture of others, for creativity—that have at most a tangential relationship with what our tests can measure.[8] In this culture, we have a hard time even finding appropriate language to talk about the size of persons' spirits, though most of us, at least, have had the experience of knowing persons whose beings seemed richer and fuller than others'. Just as we need to provide appropriate nourishment for physical growth, though the range of what is nourishing is enormous, so also we need to provide appropriate nourishment for spiritual growth across the wide spectrum of practices available to us. The power to nurture life, to create large and healthy spirits, is what I call love.

Before I move to a discussion of some of the institutional manifestations of power as control and power as life, I want to suggest that playfulness is an important feature of the moral structure of interpersonal relationships that build on the power of life and that counter power as control. Control is frustrated by play, by a delight in the intrinsic features of behavior for its own sake, whether that is repetitive and soothing, like swinging on a swing, or whether it is spontaneous and unpredictable, like playing in the spray of a hose on a warm summer day. Play is an important feature of conversation, of intimacy, even of the strategy sessions that make everyday life manageable; the point of play is not control but an experience of the richness of life.[9] Playfulness is itself subversive of control. I think of a parent whose best attempts at organizing a four year old for the day dissolve into laughter at the ensemble the child has donned for Sunday school. Such play subverts control, and it offers opportunity for rich, celebratory occasions where what is being celebrated is the being of each person and the relationship between them.

Control diminishes. Love builds up. All persons and interpersonal relationships exist within institutional structures and both shape and are shaped by them. If power as life is genuine power, it must be operative on structural levels as well.

POWER AS INSTITUTIONAL

What is the institutional face of power as control? In her book *Justice and the Politics of Difference,* Iris Marion Young describes the tentacles of oppression that grow out of a distributive paradigm

language

of justice in which justice is understood to be fair distribution of products and the metaphor of "product" is used to characterize all social goods.[10] She argues that access rather than distribution should be the fundamental mechanism and measure of justice. Collapsing genuine differences between groups and individuals into one system of production obscures the degree to which the system is itself constructed by and for the interests of a specific if elusive group. Access to the creation of the system by all affected groups must underlie any distributional considerations of the products of the system.

Young speaks of a "family of concepts of oppression" that constitute the complex phenomenon in this culture: exploitation, marginalization, powerlessness, cultural imperialism, and violence.[11] This "family" or these tentacles are the various arms of oppression that are inherent in traditional Western theories of justice and that are enacted in the institutions we have formed. For Young, if the power to control the nature of the institution, its goals and procedures, as well as its products, is not accessible to all groups coming under their operation, then distribution of its products, however fairly enacted, will not eliminate the oppressive nature of the institutions.

As helpful as her complex analysis is, it is important to note that she never moves beyond an understanding of power as control. The task is to minimize the danger of control, its potential to oppress, by sharing access to the control as widely as possible. In a move strangely reminiscent of Reinhold Niebuhr, she wants to mitigate power's intrinsic danger through political balance. Just as abuse is the inevitable outcome of power as control in interpersonal relationships, so also oppression is the institutional face of power as control. The best we can do is to let groups monitor and moderate their vulnerability to oppression.

Sharon Welch has mounted a critique of institutional power as control in a more radical way. In her book *An Ethic of Risk* she argues that even well-meaning persons are gripped by ethical paralysis in the face of the social crises that confront us. That paralysis is at least partly attributable to the dynamic of control that characterizes so much of our ethical analysis and public policy. Her primary example is the threat of nuclear war, but even as that recedes, at least for now, her fundamental insight remains valuable; control of the consequences of our deliberations and decisions ought not to be determinative for those deliberations and decisions. In the complex reality of modern institutional influence and operations, guaranteed outcomes of public policy are imaginable only through the illusion of a kind of control that extreme privilege can promise but can only erratically deliver. Welch argues that our public policy deliberations emanate from and focus on the need to control to the detriment of any genuinely effective strategies that address the concrete problems facing us. Our ethical paralysis can be overcome only by moving outside or beyond a paradigm of success and embracing an ethic of risk in which moral efficacy is as much a function of process as it is of consequence.

When the dynamic of institutional power is control, authority becomes authoritarian, access to the mechanisms of control becomes itself closely controlled, often under the guise of "protection," or "preservation," and dialogue is characterized as disagreement or even dissent.[12] The document *Malleus Maleficarum,* which was discussed in the first chapter, is a quintessential example of the institutional dynamics of control and its oppressive nature. Less obvious but no less present is the element of control in the suggestions of institutional reality that can be discerned in Ephesians. These ancient and contemporary examples all exhibit the institutional face of power as control.

As in the case of interpersonal power, we have less practice identifying and articulating the institutional face of power as life. In fact, at the institutional level, we have much less experience of this form of power, and what we have is fragmented and extracted from the overarching dynamic of control that characterizes the institutions that touch our lives. However, those experiences, rare and fleeting though they may be, can serve as proleptic instances of another structure for our common lives at the institutional level.

The Jewish feminist Marcia Falk offers what we might term a prophetic option for communal and institutional transformation. She has researched with great care the historical realities of women's participation in the formation and practices of Judaism.

She has reclaimed roles and concepts that a malestream reading of the tradition has overlooked, and she works creatively to incorporate historical tradition into contemporary practices. However, the task of historical reconstruction is difficult and at times provides a tenuous basis for a liberating hermeneutic of what has, in fact, been an oppressive tradition for women.[13] And when we get to the place where history is an inadequate resource, we turn elsewhere. As Falk so eloquently states, "What we cannot remember we must imagine." If we individually and as a people cannot remember enough about institutional power as the power of life, we must imagine it and construct it.

Other feminist scholars have suggested other forms of the "prophetic option." Letty Russell speaks of the "authority of the future,"[14] and Beverly Harrison uses the phrase "utopic envisionment."[15] What all of these feminists are pointing to in the context of their own projects is the need to move beyond our experience of oppressive institutions, using that experience to provide necessary and helpful lessons but not restricting ourselves to old structures and patterns. I certainly share the realization that our experience under oppressive conditions does not provide us with the tools we need to construct the social contexts necessary for the full release of power as life. I also share their commitment to envisioning options that we have not experienced and to experimenting with them, letting the new structures and procedures find texture in lived reality. However, I am acutely aware, as are they, of the degree to which all of us have been formed by the institutions in which our lives are inserted. We cannot shed our socialization by and to oppression like a layer of clothing. Those of us in particular who are advantaged in some ways by the oppressive system, however clear our conscious commitments may be, find that it adheres to us in subtle and sometimes not so subtle ways, and we adhere to it. We need not despair, for change can happen in human lives and spirits, but the caution must ground us in a realistic appraisal of what is possible and how hard it will be. For feminists, "utopic envisionment" is not centrally an intellectual exercise but a first step in actually restructuring human community, and we must remember that it is humans with whom we are concerned.

Knowing that we will not be able fully to outline the institutional form of power as life, what are some of its features that we can discern? First, as with interpersonal relationships, institutions must be responsive to and responsible for the concrete needs of the concrete persons for whom they exist. I will modify and refine that claim below, but for now it is important to develop it rather baldly. Institutions have many different functions that concern access to and distribution of resources. They also may have the task of defining what resources a society needs and in what proportions. Given the whole complex panoply of possibilities depending on any society's endowment of material resources, its history of their development and distribution, its political structure, its social values and formative myths, its religious heritage and practices, its technological sophistication and the relation between its technology and expressed social values, the gaps that may exist between professed social goals and actual social situations, and so on, the opportunities for oppression or enhancement of life and life chances are enormous. If life is to be enhanced by institutional power, that power must be in service of the actual lives it touches. In any society as complicated and multiplicitous as ours, a commitment to the reality of persons' lives will entail a responsibility to diversity, to "difference" in Young's terminology. Homogenizing diversity in the name of efficiency is itself oppressive because it results in the hegemonic control by one group of the social agendas of others. The first question an institution must ask itself is not "What is our task?" but "Whom do we serve?"

The use of servant language to characterize the place of institutions in our society is not unusual. "By the people and for the people" is not only a phrase in the founding documents of this country, but it is also part of the formative myth about our society that many persons, including many privileged persons, want to continue to claim. One fundamental feature of institutional power as the power of life is to concretize the slogan and insist that "the people" by and for whom the government exists are those who are really there, with the racial, social, ethnic, economic, educational realities of their lives. "The people" are not only those who actually work in the institution or those who ben-

63

efit by the institution as it is constituted, but also all those who come under its power.

The claim that institutions should serve the people with whom they actually deal must be modified by a recognition that the "reality" of the people is to a large degree formed by the institutions that help to shape their lives. Acknowledgment of a post-modern consciousness, even if one is not thoroughly postmod-ernist, eliminates the possibility of what Paul Ricoeur calls in another context a "first naiveté."[16] From Martin Heidegger to Simone de Beauvoir to Peter Berger to Alasdair MacIntyre to Michel Foucault, the literature that shapes our interpretive cate-gories instructs us in the extent to which people are products of the institutions into which they are born. Thus to claim that insti-tutions are to serve the people is a claim more about intention and attention than content. However, there are fundamental material needs, malleable but undeniable, that all persons have.[17] Furthermore, all groups need social organization, distributional mechanisms, institutions of instruction, of restraint, and so on. All of these institutions can be constituted primarily to control or to enhance life, the life of the people with whom it actually comes into contact. At the institutional level, power as control can be contrasted with power as response.

CULTURAL POWER

Following Clifford Geertz, I understand *culture* to be a shared system of meanings, assumptions about what the world is like and thus assumptions about how to interpret persons and groups, objects and events, institutions and procedures that con-stitute the world.[18] Culture may have some splendid manifesta-tions—buildings and music and dance and literature—but most of what makes up culture is "what goes without saying." Culture is largely invisible to its practitioners; it is often only the outsider who can see its contours and then must learn, with varying degrees of difficulty, the codes necessary to give what Geertz calls a "thick description" of it. The insiders often can give no descrip-tion at all without the interest and the prompting of the stranger.

The culture is the background, the Heideggerian *Lebenswelt*, what persons know in common.

Feminist scholars differ with regard to the degree of affinity between the work of Michel Foucault and the feminist projects.[19] However, what we have undoubtedly learned from him is the political nature of theory. Many feminist scholars have identified the political impact of so-called objective knowledge, but Foucault shone a spotlight on the degree to which theory shapes not only cultural assumptions and social institutions but also personal identity. One need not agree with Foucault that identity is wholly a cultural product to recognize the degree to which the dominant theories of our culture provide to a large extent the agendas for concrete human lives.[20]

Just as there is no politically innocent institution, so also there is no politically innocent cultural theory. The deepest assumptions that shape us, the interpretive categories with which we negotiate our world, are themselves liable to questions about agendas and political consequences. They are vulnerable, that is, to the ethical question about who gains and who loses from the basic assumptions of our shared lives and who is in charge of weighing the gains and losses.

In our world at this time in history, power as control at the level of culture manifests itself as hegemony. The fact about our society is that our people have different roots, different cultural lenses. Hegemonic power erases the differences, at least for those who wield the power, and/or it assigns the dominant meanings to the differences. That is, it controls the assumptions of our interactions in fundamental and often invisible ways. We are in the process of widespread cultural transitions, the depth of which it is too soon to assess. The cultural hegemony of our society is being exposed and challenged on a number of fronts. Women, people of color, gay men and lesbians, for example, not only reject some of the cultural interpretations assigned to them but provide alternative webs of meanings that emanate from and make much better sense of their experience. In this time of transition, it is as though we have the opportunity to hold a mirror to our culture, making more of it visible than is usually the case. What we are seeing is a clash between hegemony and plurality.

This clash has been labeled a contest over what is politically correct, a contest about who will control the cultural definitions. From the perspective of our study of power, this interpretation of the cultural transition in which we are engaged does not challenge hegemony but only challenges its source and extent. The contest is still over who has control of the cultural definitions and does not, therefore, provide a radical alternative to the nature of cultural power itself. It may be the case that some persons who challenge the power of our culture are doing so from the position of wanting to wrest control from those who have exercised it in order to exercise it themselves in a new hegemony. On the other hand, it may be that alternative visions are awaiting articulation and instantiation. To designate the challenge to our present culture as an issue of who is politically correct is to control the meaning of the challenge and to forestall alternative meanings even for those persons and groups who are the challengers.

The vehemence with which the challenge to shared cultural assumptions is being resisted is itself testimony to the usually unspoken sense that things are getting out of control.[21] That sense is shared by those for whom the cultural hegemony of the past provided a more or less workable meaning system. For others, of course, those whose lives were rendered anomolous by the culture, there is little resistance to change or nostalgia for a more coherent past.[22]

What might we call power as life at the cultural level? How might we envision it? In our world it would be constituted by multiplicity; the fundamental mechanism of power as life at the cultural level in our society is hospitality, not control. It is characterized by openness to difference, by dialogue among different constitutive narratives of the past and present, by accessibility to and choice among those narratives. Culture itself will be fluid, multiple, literally out of control. For example, the narratives we tell about who we are and who we were will be inclusive of many different kinds of experiences. There would not be one history to which we could appeal. In fact, there never has been; rather, a partial story has masqueraded as the whole. If culture reflects and enhances the genuine variety of meaning structures that are both possible and necessary in our society, several stories will be told at once, and only in the fullness of their several tellings will the whole culture's story be found.

As history will be constituted by several narratives, so will the other myths of our culture function in their particularity. Feminist scholars in psychology and philosophy, for example, have exposed the male bias in the ways we have constituted and described identity, though there is certainly no unanimity regarding the most adequate use and effect of gender analysis in this or any other field of inquiry.[23]

If one operates with a deeply ingrained sense that power *is* control, as all of us in this society must to some extent, then the prospect of a culture fueled by hospitality is to some degree both terrifying and incomprehensible. Certainly it is the case that we have less experience with power as life at the cultural level than we do at the personal and even the institutional level. However, the logic and the poetry of "the other face of power" suggests a direction for us to go.

THEOLOGICAL POWER

There is sufficient evidence in Scripture, tradition, and the practices of churches to support a case that the nature of God's power is properly characterized as control. The scriptural source I used above is Ephesians 5; there are many options from early to later writings in the canon. The first creation story can be read as a story about God wresting control of chaos and shaping it to God's ends. Many of the scriptural images of God suggest a figure of control, among them King, Almighty Father, Lord, Commander, and Judge. God is petitioned to bring control to human lives, relationships, institutions, and cultures. The doctrine of divine providence is in part, at least, an articulation of our confidence that God is in control of history, personal and corporate. Attributes that the classical Christian tradition associates with God—omnipotence, omniscience, and omnipresence—all resonate with an understanding of God's power as control.

There are other images, other voices, other claims.[24] I have already contrasted I Corinthians 1 with Ephesians 5, and I will say much more about I Corinthians 1 in the next chapter. The first creation story can be read as the power of life bursting forth in glorious profusion. There are images of God as Lover; as tender, nurturing Parent, both Father and Mother; as Servant; as Healer; as Friend. There are theological claims that God is partner with humanity in the ongoing creation of life. There are petitions for the presence of God in the midst of suffering and death. There is the process of life itself, vibrant, unpredictable, delightful, painful, always changing. Process theology, creation theology, liberation theology, and feminist theology have all mounted doctrinal challenges to the classical formulations of the characteristics of God that would associate God with control, and with those in control.

If God's power is not that of control, if it is understood as the power of life, then the Christian story gets read differently, told differently, heard differently, and it provides different warrants for structuring our lives together on interpersonal, institutional, and cultural levels. We are to be about the business of loving each other into being in the context of trust and accessibility within a culture of hospitality that affirms life in partnership with God.

Does the central symbol of the Christian faith, the cross of Jesus Christ, support or contradict a claim that power as life, as love, is not controlling and that it presents a viable alternative center for the structuring of human community? It is to that question we now turn.

CHAPTER FOUR

THE POWER OF THE CROSS

The Christian Bible is not so much a portrait of God as it is a mosaic of God, and not all the pieces fit together to present a singular, consistent picture.[1] The images of God, the stories of God and God's interactions with God's people, are multifarious enough to support any number of theological/ethical claims regarding the nature of God and the normative shape of human life, and they have been so used. I have no illusions about finding a definitive presentation of God's nature and therefore of God's power and mounting a decisive argument to settle the matter once and for all. I have chosen and will describe just one presentation that emerges from and is ringed around with theological arguments and insights and that comes from a central Christian scriptural source: Paul's first letter to the community at Corinth.[2] In the next chapter I will argue that the contemporary feminist Christian conception of power as eroticism, or the power of life, offers the best hermeneutic of Paul's understanding of the power of the cross. Given the feminist Christian interpretation, the power of the cross offers a powerful resource for the normative features of contemporary Christian community.

PAUL'S PROJECT: CREATING CROSS-SHAPED COMMUNITIES

Whatever the actual historical events that marked his conversion, the record leaves no doubt that Saul who became Paul was devoted to the project of proclaiming the gospel and of gathering together groups of people into communities that attempted to live out the message they heard proclaimed.[3] That is, Paul's project did not find completion in the proclamation itself, however foundational and central to his mission proclamation was. Rather, there seems to have been something about the content of the gospel that demanded its enactment in the lives of the persons who heard it, not just individually but also in community. The stories in Acts suggest a kind of religious contagion that seemed to characterize the telling of the story of Jesus the Christ, an impulse to spread the word that came from within the believers and that operated apart from the different versions of Jesus' commands at the end of three of the Gospel accounts. Spreading the gospel is depicted as something that persons *wanted* to do as well as something they *ought* to do. However, from the letters of Paul we learn most directly and in most detail about the community-building enterprise, the attempt to structure lives together such that the message of the gospel was not only proclaimed to those who had not heard it but also was lived out in the everyday activities of those who had. The gospel message itself, then, formed a creative normative center for human community. Given Paul's eschatological expectations and those of other early Christians, the hard work of forming and maintaining—and correcting—human community may appear to be a surprising response to the gospel. If the return of Christ and the end of the world were immanent, why would Paul and others struggle so hard and argue so much about how life in Christ is to look in its *communal* dimensions? The anthropological/cultural response is that human life is communal; that is certainly the case for first-century Jewish and Greco-Roman persons. The theological/ethical response is that there is something about the gospel message that finds full expression only in community, at least in Paul's version of it.

RESOCIALIZATION AND CHRISTIAN COMMUNITY

Borrowing a term from contemporary sociology, it is helpful to think of Paul's communal project as that of resocializing persons into communities with a specifically Christian ethos.[4] That is, he was not concerned solely with shaping behaviors, though concrete ethical injunctions certainly play a role in Paul's correspondence. He also, however, grounded his ethical advice in what he assumed, hoped, and argued should be the shared perceptions of reality that provided the context and meaning of his ethics. We can say, then, that along with the normative standards by which the communities should be structured, Paul attempted to provide the contours of the symbolic world within which the communities would live.

Resocialization, of course, is a secondary process that must interact with the primary socialization that everyone undergoes. All persons in the early Christian communities, including Paul, had been socialized into families, associations of many kinds, religions, and some elements of a shared culture, and there were aspects of those loyalties, values, perceptions of reality that they would have to renounce in order to become a part of the developing Christian ethos. Social theory tells us that persons who undergo voluntary resocialization are likely to have experienced "cognitive dissonance" prior to their resocialization.[5] Research into the social reality of early Christian communities indicates that their members exhibited features of social dislocation or "status inconsistency" such that it is likely they experienced cognitive dissonance.[6] The experiential gap between the social reality that was supposed to exist and the social reality of their actual lives would plausibly work to make them receptive to a new social reality, including a new meaning structure, that made better and more complete sense out of their experience. "A proposal for a new social reality built upon a new meaning structure" is a good description of Paul's ethics of community. Paul's role was teacher, leader, guide, and sometimes a figure of intense dispute in the process of resocialization within a new symbol system that provided a meaning structure, a lived reality, that promised to be more adequate than those that were left behind. And central to the new meaning system was what Paul spoke about as "the power of the cross."[7]

Resocialization is an ongoing process, one that usually does not transpire smoothly and evenly. Various aspects of the new symbol system and way of life will be more or less accessible, more or less compelling, more or less manageable. Furthermore, there will always be overlap between the old symbol system and the new, between old and new ways of perceiving and behaving.[8] Paul's correspondence provides for us windows, however smudged, through which to view some of the problems and disputes that resocialization into a Christian ethos occasioned.

For all of the opacity occasioned by the intervening centuries and by the state of our sources, it is clear that for Paul, at least, the cross of Jesus Christ provided the center of the new symbol system around which he attempted to form communities. At the heart of any community is its understanding and practice of power; at the heart of the "new world" Paul was both proclaiming and helping to create is the power of the cross. What did he mean and how did the power of the cross function in his communal ethics?

THE POWER OF THE CROSS

While the cross plays a central role in Paul's letters, we find a condensed discussion in I Corinthians 1:18-31. It is to be expected that a community in the process of formation would be concerned about issues of social power, and the Corinthian correspondence is full of such disputes. There is, however, no indication that the Corinthians questioned or objected to a commonly held concept of power. Yet Paul raises the question of the *nature* of power at key points in the letters, one of which we will examine in depth. He is concerned to reshape perceptions of power according to what he understood to be the import of the central symbol of the new Christian ethos: the cross.

In chapter 1 I defined power in general very neutrally as "the ability to accomplish desired ends" (see p. 20). In the first century as now, if the issue of the nature of power is not raised, it is common to assume that the ability to achieve one's ends involves force of some kind—physical, psychological, spiritual; important desired ends will not be held in common, and the fulfillment of one group's ends will mean the political suppression of others'. Factions result and power struggles can ensue; Paul's reflections on the meetings in Jerusalem and Antioch in Galatians, as well as textual evidence in the Corinthian correspondence, suggest that power struggles were taking place in and among the early Christian communities.

There are a number of options for interpreting and managing these contests for power that do not challenge the underlying assumption that the nature of power is forceful control of another or others to accomplish one's desired ends. Paul makes the much more radical move of redefining power in terms of the cross of Jesus Christ. Paul insists that insight into the true nature of reality as it is embodied in the cross is indispensable for grasping and enacting the true reality of Christian life as embodied in Christian communities. The *is* of the cross of Christ is both the ground and the source of the *ought* of Christian community, including its understanding and embodiment of power. Let us look again at the text.

I CORINTHIANS 1:18-31

Paul's description of the power of God in I Corinthians 1:18-31 proceeds by way of a group of antitheses and grammatical equivalences. The word of the cross (1:18) is opposed to the wisdom of the world (1:21). Within these two epistemological categories stand two groups of people: those who are being saved and those who are perishing (1:18). For the first group, the cross is the power of God; for the second group, it is folly, a stumbling block. The two groups of people are delineated and defined by their response to the "word of the cross." (Note that both groups include Jews and Gentiles; the group boundaries are ethnically indifferent.)

Besides the oppositional discussion, Paul gives positive content to "the word of the cross" in this text. As we saw, it is to be understood as the power of God (1:18). In addition, it is said to yield salvation (1:21), to be the wisdom of God (1:22), and by implication, it yields knowledge of God (1:21). The cross, then, is powerful, wise, rich in knowledge.

The efficacy that Paul posits for the cross in terms of the claims, goals, and desires of this religious community leaves no doubt that the cross is only apparently folly—and only folly to those who are themselves foolish. In other words, to understand the cross as folly is to reveal a basic misunderstanding of the structures of reality, including, of course, human community. Thus Paul is *not* granting that the perception of the cross as folly is a reasonable conclusion given an alternative, but plausible, reality structure and system of meanings. Rather, he is indicting any other "sacred canopy"[9] because the one under which he stands provides the only location from which to perceive the centrality and meaning of the cross. It is precisely a misperception of the cross that reveals the inadequacy of any other symbol system; in this argument, Paul makes the cross the fulcrum and the measure of reality itself.

What is the understanding of power against which the power of the cross would appear to be folly? It is, of course, a conception of power as control, of force, of efficacy over others. The cross represented for Paul and represents for us utter lack of control, the inversion of force, a deep and astounding failure to achieve one's own ends, if we understand success to be characterized by victory even at the price of violence. If one understands power as control, the cross represents victimization, loss of power, defeat. However, that is precisely the interpretation that Paul rejects. For him the cross is the central symbol of the power of God, a power that no one could seriously characterize as weakness or folly.[10]

How can the cross symbolize the power of God? It can do so only if we reject an interpretation of power as control. It can do so only if wisdom and knowledge of God do not depend on the unchangeable, controlling images of God that so much of the Christian tradition has espoused. It can do so only if we allow it to pose as serious a hermeneutical challenge to our understanding of power and reality as it did for Paul.

The power of God in the cross is not the power to die but the power to live. It is power that does not try to control events to affect one's will but rather power that brings forth life even from the desolation of defeat and death. The power of the cross is not the crucifixion but the resurrection—surprising, astonishing, utterly unpredictable.

In I Corinthians 15 Paul puts forth the only sustained discussion of individual resurrection in the whole New Testament. It is eloquent but finally not conclusive in any concrete way as his attempts to give a satisfactory description finally appeal to the category of mystery (15:51ff.). The fact that "believers" are resurrected is important to Paul; *how* that happens remains shrouded in speculation. The resurrection of Jesus as the Christ, however, finds concrete expression not only in the post-resurrection appearances but also in the lives of the communities that comprise "the body of Christ" as they seek to live out the power of the cross, which is not controlling but life-giving. Long after the post-resurrection appearances have become secondhand stories, the communities who gather around the symbol of the cross embody in ongoing ways the power of God manifest in the cross-shaped communities.

For Paul, the reality of the risen Christ is not reducible to the lives of the communities to whom he was still present. However, the communities were the ongoing embodiment of the risen Christ in the world, the places in which the Christ is manifest in the world. He spoke of living temples; that metaphor moves toward literal description of the ongoing presence of Christ.

As I mentioned above, one of the most persistent, and in many ways appealing, Christian heresies is Docetism, the inability to hold together the divinity and the humanity of Jesus and the decision, or inclination, to let his humanity be trumped if not overshadowed by his divinity.[11] Some version of Docetism can mar our grasp of Paul's understanding of the nature of Christian community. Christian community was to enact, live out, embody the values, visions, symbol system that the risen Christ embodied, with the power of the cross at the center of that new world. The communities themselves, then, could be said to be both human and divine, enacting in human life the "mind of Christ," a God's-eye perception of reality, the logos of the cross.[12] They were to be what God intended for human life, and part of what God intended is that human community be in close partnership with God, experiencing in its own interactions the love and life of God. The communities were confronted with both amazing opportunity and amazing responsibility; an insistence on both moves through Paul's letters like waves on a shore.

If what was at stake in the founding and structuring of Christian community around the power of the cross and its attendant values and behaviors was making manifest the risen Christ in the world, making manifest the living word of God, then the urgency of getting the perceptions right, the structures right, the values right, is clear and justified. For Paul, finally, all personal rivalries aside, his often eloquent, sometimes frustrated, driven, yes urgent, appeals to the "gospel of Jesus Christ and him crucified" were precisely Paul's way of insisting that if the risen Christ is to continue to be present in the world, he must be embodied by the communities. If communities were formed around any other symbolic center with any other structures and values, some other Christ would be manifest. The connection between the presence of the risen Christ and the concrete reality of the communities was that close. What was at stake, then, was an ongoing experience of *this* God, *this* love, that Paul encountered at some point in such a life-changing way.

As we saw above, at the center of it all is the "foolish" display of the power of God in the cross. Here we need to move with great care back to our discussion of I Corinthians 1:18-31 and forward to a fuller understanding of what exactly composes that power. We can then move from the nature of God's power to some of the fundamental communal structures that Paul proposed.

First, we noted above that the power of which Paul speaks is genuine power; it is the power of God that no one would seriously interpret as weakness. Whatever the nature of God's power, it is the definitive power; all else is derivative. Second, we noted that Paul contrasted it with the power of the world, and the oppositions included the abilities to see or not to see that God's power is truly power. In other words, it does not at first glance look powerful if what one is looking for is something that resembles, or models, worldly power. Third, it is the "power to save." Leaving aside all the vexed questions about the constitution of salvation, with its centuries of theological barnacles, what Paul clearly refers to here is the ongoing life of the Christ after his crucifixion and the ongoing life of persons who see and accept this God.[13] In other words, the power of the cross is the power of life. It is unexpected; we do not expect to look at death and discover life. It is ongoing; we know about the power of the cross only from the continuing presence of the risen Christ among us, and Christian communities manifest that life in the world. Elsewhere in I Corinthians, and throughout his correspondence, Paul equates the power of God and the love of God. The power of the cross is love.

The power of the cross, God's power, is *not* controlling. God did not intervene in the crucifixion, arranging events so that the power of life would violently vanquish violence or control its outcome. Violence did its worst, and love and life went on. Even the nature of that life was surprising, unexpected, not always easy to recognize as the often humorous appearance stories suggest and as Paul's vexed attempts to create unity of spirit among Christians bore out. The power of the cross, the power of God, the power of life, the power of love simply is not amenable to our categories of experience if those categories emanate from the expectations and values of control. We join many early Christians in remaining lost, confused, somehow disappointed by the gospel if what they and we want from it is better control, more power to manipulate ourselves, each other, and God.

THE NORMATIVE CONTOURS OF CRUCIFORM POWER

I noted above the close connection, if not identification, between the ongoing presence of the risen Christ in the world and the manifestation of that life in Christian community. What are the communal structures that Paul discerned and proposed as those that embody the mind of Christ? How does the risen Christ embodied in human community appear in the world?

A careful look at the Pauline correspondence allows us to identify two central normative pillars for Christian community. The first is unity. Paul commends those communities who seem to maintain unity—the Thessalonians and the Philippians—and he exhorts those who are experiencing divisions—the Corinthians, the Galatians perhaps, and the Roman community—in a more opaque way. (Do we read the Jew/Gentile contrasts as divisions or as illustrations?) Even Philemon reflects Paul's fundamental concern for the unity of persons in Christian community.

Why Paul's concern, one might even say his obsession, with unity? There are two ways to answer that question. First, one could appeal, as he does in I Corinthians and in Romans, to the unity of the risen Christ, which the "body of Christ" is to reflect. The fundamental reality that the Christian communities are to embody is the presence of the risen Christ in the world. Since Christ is not multiple, not divided, and according to Paul at least, available to all persons regardless of ethnic, religious, and social, "worldly," divisions, then divisions in the community are deeply self-contradictory. Lack of unity reflects the communities' betrayal of their center, the one God, and thus the loss of their identity as *Christian* community. Paul's insistence on unity, then, is foundational. It is an appeal to the fundamental reality of their existence as communities that embody the risen Christ.

There is, however, another way to look at the insistence on the unity of Christians that is at the heart of Christian community shaped by the power of the cross. If power is the power of life, of love, then self-interest and the interest of the other are not fundamentally in conflict. If what we are most centrally about is to foster life in all its forms, then difference does not have to be divisive. Controversy does not have to lead to division as we care as much about the well-being of the other, and the other about us, as we each do about ourselves. If what holds us together is a common love, then the best interests of each of us and of all of us is to keep that love alive.

The unity of the fundamental interests and identity of all Christians is manifest in the second normative pillar of Christian community: mutual service, or, to use Paul's metaphor, "building up." We have seen in previous chapters how understanding power as love, as life, manifests itself in our activity of loving one another into being, in building up the spirits of ourselves and those around us, concerned not to make the other less but more.[14]

Paul offers several examples of resolving conflicts based on the centrality of power as love, as life.[15] One especially vivid example comes from I Corinthians 8–10, the familiar example of dietary restrictions and Christian freedom. The Corinthian community was made up of people from different ethnic backgrounds. At least some of the Jews among them had identified with and participated in a cult that defined itself in part with dietary laws of varying degrees of strictness. At least some of the Gentiles among them had participated in pagan cults in which meat was sacrificed to idols and then eaten as participation in the reality of that god or goddess. For at least some Jews and at least some Gentiles, then, in the new Corinthian Christian community, the issue of eating meat that was sold in the local marketplace, which would very likely have been part of a pagan ritual sacrifice, was problematic. However, the gospel of Jesus Christ promised freedom from the old norms and restrictions. And Paul certainly preached a gospel of freedom. To return to language used above, persons entering Christian community were radically resocialized to a new "reality" with the power of the cross in the center. Whatever values and practices they had embodied in their lives would be subject to the new symbol system, the new perspective on life that the gospel offered. Thus theoretically, at least, those in the Corinthian community who insisted that it did not matter what they ate were taking the theologically correct stance. Dietary laws were apparently not part of the Christian cult.[16] The reality and power of the idols were denied and replaced by the power of the cross.

Paul did not, however, respond to the issue of whether or not to eat meat offered to idols based on the criterion of theological correctness. At the end of his long discussion Paul says, " 'All things are lawful,' but not all things are beneficial. 'All things are lawful,' but not all things build up. Do not seek your own advantage but that of the other" (I Cor. 10:23-24).

In this famous "Yes, but . . . " response to the Corinthians' claim to be free from the pernicious influence of idols, Paul gives content to his norm of mutual service, or building up. Seeking the good of the other person is the measure of the "lawfulness" of actions within the Christian community. If the action of eating meat at a communal meal will harm no one, then it is "legal." If, on the other hand, another community member is present at the meal, someone for whom the reality of idols has not yet been expunged from consciousness, then that same action becomes "illegal."

Within the belief structure of the Christian community, the person who denies the reality of idols is correct and the person who retains at least a residual belief in their reality is incorrect; Paul affirms the "theological" position of the former. As he says, "We know that 'no idol in the world really exists,' and that 'there is no God but one' " (I Cor. 8:4). However, the ethical priority is clear: Acting on correct belief at the expense of another person is wrong.

Unwavering insistence on the existence of the one God is a central aspect of the Christian interpretation of reality. Certainly the actual practice of idolatry is condemned by Paul in the strongest terms (e.g., I Cor. 10:14-22). Thus those to whom Paul refers as "the strong," those who deny the reality of the idols and can freely participate in the meat-eating meals, are correct about an issue that is hardly trivial. Is their theological maturity to be circumscribed by the needs of those whose understanding is not so developed?

As my paraphrase is meant to highlight, Paul's understanding of theological maturity within the Christian ethos cannot be divided off from the concrete needs of other persons in the community. The claim to theological maturity or "knowledge" by those who made it was ethically intolerable precisely because it disregarded the nature of the Christ that it purported to contain. The power that the "superior" knowledge that theological maturity represents is the power to harm and control, just the opposite of the power the Christian community is to recognize and enact. A superior theological understanding, here meaning freedom from the reality of idols, must give way before the needs of other persons even if those other persons are not able to integrate fully the theologically correct position. "Mature" Christian behavior gives priority not to those who know more but to those who need more.

SUMMARY

Paul's presentation of "the power of the cross" in I Corinthians shows forth a form of power that is life-giving, loving. It is difficult to grasp because it is so different from what the "world" presents as power, from our interpretation and experience of power as control, manipulative, and often violent. The power of the cross is unexpected, unpredictable, essentially and fundamentally out of control.

Paul envisioned the embodiment of this power in the world as community. Persons gathered together in and around the power of the cross were to be "the body of Christ," the manifestation of the risen Christ in the world, and the presentation of the power of the cross. The normative pillars of such community are unity and mutual upbuilding, norms that exercise the power of life in concrete, everyday forms.

Paul's vision was a difficult one, and as the process of institutionalization visible in later New Testament texts demonstrates, it was soon lost. Even he was not always consistently faithful to his vision, his goal, his experience of community built upon the power of life.[17] I believe, however, that it is a vision worth reclaiming and developing, difficult as it continues to be, both noetically and ontologically, to "realize" such power.

In the next chapter I will make explicit the implicit connections between Paul's understanding of power and that put forth by contemporary Christian feminists. I will argue that we are Paul's best exegetes. I will also argue that the cross is not a dangerous symbol for Christian feminism but a resource we have both the right and the obligation to restore and enact.

CHAPTER FIVE

RECLAIMING THE CROSS

The cross is a deeply problematic symbol for contemporary Christian feminists as we attempt to shape community so that power is exercised and experienced as life-giving rather than controlling and violent. In fact, the cross has functioned as the antithesis of an understanding of power as essentially erotic, essentially loving. It has come to represent the legitimation, even the glorification, of suffering, of abuse, of violence. It functions as a symbol for death, not life.

Feminist objections to the cross as a symbol of suffering are clearly articulated in *Christianity, Patriarchy, and Abuse: A Feminist Critique.* In their essay entitled "For God So Loved the World," Joanne Carlson Brown and Rebecca Parker survey the traditional interpretations of the meaning of the cross through the doctrine of atonement and compellingly conclude that the doctrine through the centuries has served to justify human suffering and abusive behavior.

Their analysis divides the history of the doctrine into classical and critical traditions. Under the first rubric they include three versions of the doctrine. The first is the "Christus Victor" tradition in which Christ's suffering is illusory because the victory was in place beforehand through the agency of a providential deity. The second is the "Satisfaction Tradition" exemplified by Anselm in which human sin is so terrible that no human act could overcome it. However, God in God's mercy sacrifices God's own son as the only price that could buy our redemption. Finally they introduce the "Moral Influence Tradition," which trades on the moral force of innocence itself and carries with it the threat that if we do not behave, someone innocent will die. They note that these characterizations of the meaning and power of the cross have implications for conceptions of the nature of God; the doctrines of God that are associated with the classical interpretations of atonement portray God as controlling and abusive.

Brown and Parker also identify a tradition of scholarship within Christianity that is critical of the classical treatments of the cross as symbolizing atonement and therefore justifying and even glorifying suffering. The first, which they call "The Suffering God," argues that the cross shows God as suffering with humanity, and that the presence of God in human suffering is itself redemptive. As a second critical stance they discuss the claims of Martin Luther King, Jr., that while suffering itself is never good, it can have good moral consequences. Persons who are oppressive can be swayed from their oppression by being confronted by human suffering in ways that other approaches cannot effect. Finally, some representatives of the liberationist tradition reject any positive aspects of suffering. It may be inevitable as we work for justice in an unjust world, but it is never salvific.

Brown and Parker find even the critical tradition to be inadequate as stances from which to overcome Christianity's penchant for glorifying suffering. In the first instance, suffering provides a point of contact, perhaps even intimacy, between God and humanity. The second instance, exemplified by the life and teachings of Martin Luther King, Jr., is a modern version of the "Moral Influence Tradition" in which suffering itself becomes a vehicle for moral persuasion in ways that other strategies cannot be. And finally, they fault even liberationists' rejection of suffering for smuggling in an element of heroism; if one is working for justice in an unjust world, one will suffer. Martyrdom carries its own spiritual power.[1]

However we may hesitate over the details of their critique, the cumulative argument they mount is a powerful one. The cross is a dangerous symbol because it issues in doctrines of atonement that glorify suffering and present a God who is sadistic, abusive, or impotent. The critique that they articulate and the revulsion that they convey are faithful representations of the sensibilities of many Christian feminist thinkers.

In *Touching Our Strength,* Carter Heyward makes similar points in different ways. There she argues for consideration and adoption of the Christa in contrast to Christ as a symbol of suffering. Unlike the male Christ, whose suffering, through the traditional doctrines, has served to justify the suffering of women, for Heyward the Christa represents all that is wrong with human suffering. Whereas for her "[Christ] has become a living symbol of our humiliation, suffering and death at the hands of christian men," the Christa represents "the erotic as power and the love of God as embodied by erotically empowered women."[2]

We can characterize the contrast Heyward is making as that between the male Christ whose suffering represents oppressive, controlling, harmful power and the female Christa whose suffering challenges control with eroticism. The male Christ is intransigently and inextricably immersed in centuries of a tradition of the hermeneutics and practice of power as control. Furthermore, the contemporary location of Christian feminist practice is, as Heyward puts it, "a fiercely misogynist, erotophobic spirituality."[3] The very shock we experience when we see a cruciform female figure calls forth both our outrage at the suffering of women in the name of Christ and at the same time the exhilaration of freedom from the old oppressive structures that are one aspect of the power of eroticism.

Can we move from here to the cross as a symbol not of death but of life, not of atonement but of the playful power of eroticism? If so, why would we want to? What is gained by reclaiming in another form a symbol that has unarguably functioned so dangerously for so long? These are the questions that any contemporary Christian feminist argument for such a move must confront. Can the cross function for us, now, as a symbol of life, and what does it give us that is of value for our lives together here and now?

I wish to deal with these questions in three steps. First, I want to address the theoretical, hermeneutical issue of the cross as a symbol of power. Is "atonement" the only or the best interpretation of its meaning for human life? What about Paul's claims about the power of the cross? How do contemporary Christian feminist claims function to exegete the cross?

Second, I will discuss the social context that is necessary for the cross to function as liberating and empowering in the lives of all for whom it is a meaningful symbol. We surely cannot simply decide in the privacy of our studies, or our hearts, that the cross is important and therefore centuries of doctrinal and historical barnacles will suddenly and miraculously fall away. We must take very seriously the damage that the cross has done and address carefully the social context in which it could function differently.

Finally, I will take up the question of what is gained by reclaiming the cross as a symbol of Christian feminist community. Included in my discussion will be some consideration about how the appellations *Christian* and *feminist* work together to establish conceptual and practical boundaries that neither alone can necessarily posit.

THE CROSS AS THE POWER OF GOD

What would it mean for contemporary Christian communities to take I Corinthians 13 as their power base? What would it mean for our lives together if we really believed that love is power, the most powerful power there is?

Christian communities were never quite able to do that. Even the Pauline correspondence, where the concept of God's power as generative and life-giving finds one of its most eloquent expressions, is replete with references and images to Christ as the paschal lamb of God whose sacrifice negotiated our salvation. That is to say, Paul's letters include a sense, though not nearly a theory, of atonement in which God requires pain and suffering as the price for God's gracious favor, and only the Christ was good enough and pure enough to pay that price. Thus even Paul, with his eloquent appeals to the power of love, leaves love and violence standing side by side as partners in the dance of life.[4]

There is, then, no trustworthy blueprint in the tradition for a communal Christian ethic that remains faithful to the insight that God's power is life-giving love. What are we to do with the tradition if we understand that insight to be central to the reality of Christian community? We must choose between the insight and the enactments. We must claim either a truth or a history, knowing, of course, that we are shaped by the history even if we choose to renounce it.

I have been building a case for choosing the insight, and I have argued indirectly for what I shall now claim openly: Contemporary Christian feminists with their emphasis on power as eroticism are the best exegetes of that insight.[5] If we are truly to take with utter seriousness Paul's claim that God's power is represented by all that our ordinary understandings of power would deem foolish, then we must move well beyond his inconsistent but predictable references to the atonement of Christ and explore the life that communities built upon and in the power of love have to offer. The *vision* of communities built on love is nicely articulated by Paul. The *development and instantiation* of that vision await further work. Contemporary Christian feminists are, first, identifying the issue of power as a central issue for any analysis and development of communal ethics, and, second, suggesting conceptions of power that are to be contrasted with power as control, manipulation, or domination. We have a chance now to do what Paul began: resocialize persons into communities where power is identified and enacted as love in a process both noetic and concrete and at the same time very simple and very difficult.

THE CROSS AS A RESOURCE

Given all the problems with the cross as a symbol of the glorification of suffering in all the forms Christianity has done that, why reclaim it as a central symbol for Christian community? Given the way in which the cross has been used through the centuries to justify abusive behaviors of all sorts, of which women have been the frequent, though not exclusive, victims, why not follow Carter Heyward and replace it with something else? Why try to reclaim the cross?

Fundamentally the cross represents the astonishing reality that God's power is not controlling. Fundamentally the cross shows God's power standing silently by while violence does its worst, while rage is unleashed in the world in paroxisms of attempts to control the religious, ethical, and social structures of life. Fundamentally the cross shows God not in armed combat with the forces of evil, as so much Christian imagery would have it, but rather it shows God quietly, deeply, almost imperceptibly changing the terms of the conflict. The cross shows us that armed conflict with the forces of evil is precisely *not* the way to image God's power, a power that is not simple acquiescence but rather the generative power of life in *all* situations. God resets the terms of violent conflict, and the terms are loving.

Just as the cross is not a violent symbol, so also it is not a passive one. It does not show us a God who stands by and lets violence win. It shows us a God who will not let violence win because God does not engage that particular contest. Rather, in the midst of the worst that violence can do, love creates life.

We need to reclaim the cross because it symbolizes the power of God as life and love. As we saw in chapter 3, power has several dimensions. We cannot reconstruct Christian community with an alternative conception of power and leave intact centuries of concepts and images and doctrines that make God's power controlling. We cannot claim the freedom and playfulness of eroticism in our own lives without admitting it in God's as well. We must challenge the hard crust of control that has grown up around the presentation and practice of the power of God in Christian communities. Ironically, our most powerful tool is the cross itself, stark, empty, an instrument of death that denies death in its transfiguration into new life, life that both symbolically and actually seems vague, somewhat unreal, certainly different from what we ordinarily know and experience.

Can we tolerate the cross as an authority for feminist Christian community? Put in other words, can we learn to trust the cross, trust that it will not hurt us but will affirm and support our lives and loves? I believe that question asks in another form whether we can trust that the power of God, that the power of life, the power of love, is really power. The question of the authority of the cross is related to the question of the nature of power itself. The power of life has not, after all, done much to protect us against violence and abuse through the centuries. If the cross is a trustworthy symbol of the power of God, then God's power is *not* controlling. Is it truly life-giving? Can the cross represent something we can trust, can rely on even in the face of various contemporary versions of the *Malleus Maleficarum?*

Questions about the cross, then, cannot be reduced to questions about the history of the use of the symbol. As problematic as that history may be, it simply invites another level of questioning. What *is* God's power? Can we trust it? We know it will not protect us from violence and abuse. Is that tolerable? Has the cross become a symbol of violence and control because that is what we need to believe about the nature of God's power? Can we really trust love? Even in the face of control? Even in the face of violence and abuse?

The cross does not justify suffering, and the cross does not deny it. There is no way to forget or erase the connection between love and suffering when the cross symbolizes the power of God. Suffering is a by-product of love. That is a fact, a terrible, horrible, never justifiable fact, but a fact nonetheless. In contrast to Parker and Brown, I think that this is the stance of contemporary liberation theologies with regard to suffering, a bluntly realistic appraisal of what happens when our lives are open one to another. If love, not manipulation or control, characterizes the connection between us, then your pain will touch me, along with your joy. I have no agenda for you to follow as the condition under which I am connected to you. There is no requirement that you be happy, content, and at peace in order for us to be in relationship. Suffering *is*. Love is stronger.

The cross is a good resource for giving us access to the power of God as love. It is not a good resource for explaining the cluster of questions that we term *theodicy*. The cross says very little to us about "why"—why violence, why pain and suffering, why lack of control, why so much love? It simply stands as a witness to these realities, which cannot be explained but can be lived. It

89

strikes me that the doctrines of atonement in their various forms are precisely attempts to answer questions that the cross as a symbol of God's power does not ask, and does not give answers to. They are not bad questions; theodicy haunts us. However, we must look elsewhere for the answers, or learn to live with the questions. If we learn to trust the cross as a resource, as a symbol of the power of God that is not controlling but is trustworthy, then we are constantly called back from the temptation to think that because God does not control, God is impotent. The cross as a symbol claims that goodness and power are *not* opposites. It is only when we continue to image and trust that power must be controlling to be powerful that we have to posit a contradiction between power and goodness. Understanding power as love, as life, changes the terms of the conversation.

Finally, the cross is a resource as we find our vision of power as love moving in and out of focus and as we find our attempts to structure our lives together in radically new ways more or less efficacious. It can serve as a kind of anchor in the midst of what often can feel like chaos. It reminds us that our project of resocializing persons into communities based on the power of love is a project of claiming the life God has for us. It helps us to trust our vision even as we try to live it out.

As Paul taught and as Christians through the ages have discovered, the *power* of the power of love can be known only by being experienced. Ontological realization precedes noetic realization. We can articulate only so much of love; even the classic eloquence of I Corinthians 13 can only indicate, evoke, recall an experiential dimension that is not totally available to cognition.[6] Furthermore, as Paul taught and as Christians through the ages have discovered, we can know *God* only as we experience God. Wisdom about God is not fundamentally cognitive but experiential, not fundamentally spoken but lived. There are edges, dimensions of the reality of God even as we can experience it that simply evade our best attempts to capture them in words. Doctrines must always whisper, never shout.

It is the escapable, unexpected, playful, irrepressible aspects of God's power, God's being that require a category such as eroticism, both for our understanding and for our experience of

God. God is out of control. God is powerful. God takes our breath away. God is passion, in passion, passionate, not primarily in spasms of suffering as classical theory would have it but in spasms of loving.

It is odd that the Christian tradition has chosen to focus on the physical suffering of Jesus as the centerpiece of the "passion story." It is certainly the case that he died a horrible death. However, the Gospel accounts of his "suffering and death" actually focus on a process of greater and greater isolation of Jesus, on a process of betrayal that Judas acts out most directly but in which all the apostles participate. Even God, perhaps, is absent when Jesus is most in need of the comfort and intimacy of that relationship. The suffering of Jesus is only partly physical; it is largely the suffering of love betrayed, seemingly inadequate to sustain life in the face of violence and death. It is the result of more and more desperate attempts to control a volatile political situation in first century C.E. Palestine. Jesus' suffering, in other words, is the multidimensional enactment of the apparent breakdown of love, of the playful erotic joy that characterized so much of his life. Even Paul's accounts of Jesus' death, sparse and atonement-centered as they are, do not focus on his physical suffering. And Paul's accounts of his own physical suffering do not glorify it but rather hold it up to show that even it does not nullify the power of the gospel. It is an inevitable by-product of the attempt to restructure life around the power of love.[7]

Why, then, do centuries of Christian teaching highlight the physical suffering of Jesus? That is a question that has no determinate textual answer. The emphasis on the physical suffering of Jesus is an oddity not accounted for by the stories in the Gospels and Paul's brief summaries. The stories focus on the immeasurably painful and utterly terrifying process of the apparent disintegration of all connectedness, of all relationships, friends, disciples, even God. The agony was over the loss not just of life, physical life, but of love. It looked as if control would destroy love.

If we want to control God, and/or if we want to image and experience God's power as controlling, then using eroticism to characterize the power of God is intolerable, shocking, even repulsive. If, however, we accept and trust that God's power is love, that the cross is about life and not death, then eroticism or something like it is necessary to talk about the power of God and the experience of God in human community. We need to capture the spontaneity, the unpredictability, the sheer irrepressible joy and abundance of life that characterizes the power the cross symbolizes. The cross, then, represents not primarily a cry of pain, though that is not silenced, but the exuberance of life as it breaks free from the control and violence it has confronted and moved through.

THE CROSS AS A BOUNDARY AND GUIDE

In addition to being a conceptual and ethical resource for Christian community, the cross as a symbol of the power of God can act as a restraint on the claims and practices of Christian community. The cross, and a conception of the power of God as life, as love, does not generate anything like a complete communal ethic. However, it does entail some ethical requirements, some contours for the shape of Christian community.

First, the cross is inclusive. Love, life, the power of God are not subject to the control or manipulation of any group of people, though many try. The power of God is universally available and never subject to exclusive control. The implication for Christian feminism of this feature is that it cannot be separatist. I have argued for and continue to argue for the possibility of separatism as a strategy for Christian feminists legitimately to employ to achieve equality, or simply to give us a respite from the struggle against sexism, but it cannot be a long-term goal. On the whole and in the long run, Christian community must be open to men as well as to women, and to persons of all races, ages, ethnicities, and sexual orientations. Separatism is an option for secular feminism, but not for Christian community.[8]

Second, any community formed around the power of the cross is dramatically and deeply inconsistent if its practice and understanding of power are controlling, manipulative, and violent. The cross provides a powerful critical tool to turn inward on the communities that exist. If their understanding and practice of power are not consonant with the power of God, then on a fundamental level they are not being faithful to the gospel of Christ. The cross is also a constant check against the use of violence to promote Christian ends, however lofty or valuable.[9] That claim is equally true on the personal, interpersonal, and communal levels.

The cross also acts as a check on the impulse to define sin as a particular form of oppression. Contrary to the claims of Brown and Parker, sin cannot be equated with patriarchy or with any "ism."[10] If the power of God is love, life, erotic play, the opposite of control, then sin is to be understood as the incapacity to trust the power of love and thus the necessity to try to control relationships with and the behavior of others. Sin may sometimes be manifest as the attempt to control life itself if one has the social resources even to imagine that. Sin, in this view, is not a set of inappropriate or illegal or immoral behaviors but the odd incapacity to love, to choose love, to trust love. Sin is the inexplicable breakdown of the process of mutual upbuilding, of loving one another into being, that constitutes the experience of the power of God in human life. Sin is the painful, frustrating, damaging process of wanting to heal—oneself or another or a relationship—and of continuing to wound and to be wounded. Sinful patterns of relating develop with the best of intentions and the worst of results. Malice, ill will, can usually be diagnosed, psychologically and spiritually. Good will that never quite manages to be expressed and embodied is a mystery. We can mean so well and do so ill. We can want so much to love and encounter our sheer incapacity in this place, at this time, to do so. We want to be supporters of one another, and find ourselves to be betrayers.

Our response to this incapacity is often that of trying to control. We may try to control ourselves, to push through the hard walls of mistrust and bad habits intractably present. Sometimes that is possible, and we can once again claim the capacity for life, for joy. Often enough, however, repeated attempts result in repeated failure and greater and greater frustration and pain, and we reach outside ourselves and try to control those around us, and perhaps the world around us. Then trust in the process of love is relinquished, replaced by an escalating, frantic, manipulative approach to life itself. It is the case that when love fails, the most loving thing to do can be simply to let go, and go on, not without guilt and regret and sheer sorrow at our inability to do what we want so badly to do.

The cross reminds us of our incapacity to love, to live, and it reminds us of our ever-present capacity to betray. It also reminds us of the power of life, of love, to change the terms of the conflict, to bring life out of the ravages of violence and destruction that are so often the result of our "power." The cross reminds us of how isolated we can be, even when what we want most is to be connected. It also reminds us of the ever-present possibility of the restoration of life, of love, even of play and joy when we can be open to the power of life and trust that love is indeed powerful. It symbolizes the worst isolation and the greatest restoration of relatedness that it is possible to imagine.

THE SOCIAL CONTEXT: CRUCIFORM COMMUNITY

It is not enough to rearticulate the meaning of the cross in the privacy of our own studies and then go about using it as though 2,000 years of oppressive history had not happened. In the first place, the symbol of the cross as it was explicated by Paul was never meant to function detached from a particular community. It was in the concrete life of the community that the symbol's power was experienced and realized. Second, the process of resocialization in which Paul was engaged is precisely the process of internalizing, personally and communally, the reality of the power of the cross as life, as love, in stark contrast to the common understanding and experience of power as control. In the first two chapters, I evoked and drew the two different faces of power. How much more clearly control can be kept in focus, can be encountered, can be believed to be powerful. It is only in the process of living another way, with another center, that we can come to trust the power of life, of God, that is not controlling but generative. Our minds will never really grasp what our lives renounce. The ability to reclaim the cross as a symbol of life-giving power is a function of the ability to live in communities that enact that power.[11] Conversely, the ability to reclaim the cross as a symbol of life-giving power enables the formation of such communities.

We must never ignore history; we also need not accede to it. The way things have been is not necessarily the way things must continue to be. The cross as our window into another possibility for human community offers feminist Christians both an invitation and an obligation to try in this century and in this society to live out that possibility.[12]

I have been arguing throughout this book that alongside the oppressive understanding and practice of power in the Christian tradition stands another vision, another conceptualization and manifestation of power that Paul began to articulate, most clearly in I Corinthians, and that contemporary feminist Christians are developing. Furthermore, I have argued that for Christians the cross is a symbol of that life-giving power, a claim that God's power is not controlling and manipulative and violent but rather creative in the face of all that. Given the deeply ambiguous nature of our tradition, contemporary Christians cannot simply retrieve a more pristine past and read off values and norms for our communities. In chapter 3 I cited Marcia Falk's claim that in the construction of healthy, healing communities, "what we cannot remember we must imagine." There is much that we need that we cannot remember; imagination is an important ingredient in Christian ethics. On the other hand, power as life, as love, can function both as a starting place and as a goal for communal ethics. If power as love, as life, as eroticism, is our center, what are some of the features of our lives together that we can discern from here?

First, we can affirm the value and the safety of diversity. In a simple, if very difficult, move, we can notice that if the point is not control, if power is seen as other-enhancing without cost to the self, then there is no need to try to make everyone the same. Diversity is frightening only in an atmosphere of control. Differences threaten because the operative mechanism of power is control. Replace control with life, with eroticism, with a fundamental dynamic of "building up" the other, then difference simply is, and is not a problem.

I am not here arguing for a simple liberal live-and-let-live ethic. Within cruciform community, diversity will bring change. Persons are loved into being by others; who those others are will affect the nature of each of us. If I spend a lot of my time and energy in a racially mixed community in this culture, I will be a different person from the one I would be were I to spend all my time with white, middle-income people, and conversely. Diversity does bring about change.

Change, personal and communal, is itself part of the process of life. When our attention is directed by and at control, change is threatening. Resistance to diversity is almost always a barricade against change. Since life itself is a process of change and change again, we are always confronted with the futility of preventing it, and the resulting frustration can lead to violence of all sorts.

If we understand power as life, eroticism, not within our control but sustaining us, then we realize that the exercise of power is not a zero-sum game. I do not lose power when you gain it. We do not share power that somehow must be divided, but rather we experience it synergistically. The greater your being, the greater the being of the community of which we are both a part. I am enhanced as you are.

Paul speaks of this dynamic with the phrase "building one another up." The mutual upbuilding that functions as a central ethical injunction in his epistles recognizes that mutual service goes beyond simple reciprocity to the synergistic enhancement of both individuals and community. As we love one another into being, we are all of us enlarged—to use a spatial metaphor—and our capacity to grow and love is itself enlarged as we experience more and more fully the presence of God and the power of the cross in our relationships.

The power of God, of life, of love does not control the negative and painful events of life. It does not insure against disaster; it will not fend off violence; it will not protect against decay and death. We must moment by moment peel away centuries' thick layers of expecting God to control life as we learn to experience and exercise another kind of power in and among ourselves. There is enormous risk in embracing the diversity and change that power as life requires of us. We may in fact feel bereft of all we hold dear, including God. Paul taught and I have argued that the only way to "know" power as life, as love, is to live it, to experience it. It must be enacted in our communities, fitfully, with mistakes, but with great determination and conviction. Our "knowledge" of God, and of life and one another, is not finally available through intellectual knowledge but only in the lived wisdom of other-directed communities. To use classical Christian terminology, incarnation precedes articulation.

Alongside the value and enactment of diversity, cruciform community operates with unity, not separation, as its fundamental state. That is to say, the task is not to overcome primal separation and somehow to achieve unity. Rather, the community is already unified by a common love of God and by a realization that the core of its life together springs from and depends on connection. Unlike *jouissance*, which operates on the edges of the symbolic, the free play of eroticism recognizes, embraces, and serves to expand connection that is to be discovered, not created. We are connected in life-giving ways, however our social structures and culturally dictated priorities may try to deny the unity. Think of the discomfort even among a group of strangers at the wailing of an infant. The discomfort may range from compassion to annoyance to something close to rage, but we are touched. The cry that is designed by life itself to get our attention, to announce need, however inchoate, is virtually universally effective. We all hate to hear a baby cry; that is the point. The connection we have with adults is often not as accessible because it is not as primitive. We have been taught or we have taught ourselves to cushion the connections. However, they are not absent and can be retrieved.

Unlike *jouissance*, the power of the cross is not gender specific. The unity that we both recognize and enact in Christian community, based on the power of the cross and our common love, precludes separatism of any sort, between the genders, the races, the classes. We cannot take the secular option of separating from persons and groups that oppress us, however appealing that option may appear. Rather, we must find ways to interact that affirm our diversity, including differing historical experiences and group memories, while at the same time remaining connected. Neither diversity nor unity can be collapsed into the other. Cruciform community is diverse, it is unified, and it is other-directed. Furthermore, it is other-directed in radical ways. In her book *Unruly Practices: Power, Discourse, and Gender in Contemporary Social Theory,* Nancy Fraser discusses several kinds of discourses about needs that have arisen in our society.[13] Among her other points she argues that the way needs get defined and by whom directly relates to the satisfaction of needs. She uses as an example the development of a battered women's movement in this country in the 1970s. Prior to this wave of feminism, wife-beating was not understood to be a political issue. "Linguistically it was classed with the disciplining of children and servants as a 'domestic'—as opposed to a 'political'—matter. Then feminist activists renamed the practice with a term drawn from criminal law and created a new kind of public discourse."[14] "Beating," a private affair, became "battering," a public one. The identification of the need was undertaken by those who understood it best, those who experienced it.

Any cruciform community will have to embody its other-directed commitments at the level of discourse as well as at the level of practice because the one serves in part to determine the other. It is at the level of discourse, as well as at the level of institutional and interpersonal interaction, that power as life must replace power as control. We must not try to speak for one another but rather remain alert to the ways in which language itself must constantly shift, change, bend to enfold new voices and new articulations of need.

Rebecca Chopp argues that fundamental to the nature of the Christian church is openness to new ways of speaking, new ways of proclaiming freedom. She writes:

> In this way to proclaim the Word to and for the world is not to claim a secure end, a final subject, a clear language, a determined politics, but precisely to open up the possibilities to live and move in the complexities, ambiguities, and richness of language, subjectivity, and politics. It is to speak forth of continual union and separation, incarnation and diffusion, in the emancipatory process of new life that both is and is to come.[15]

The creative, life-giving nature of "the Word," as Chopp uses the term, requires us to relinquish control, to reject the hegemony of discourse that is so startlingly exemplified by the *Malleus Maleficarum* and some uses of Scripture itself, and to allow the changing and transformative realities of various persons and groups to speak for themselves, and thereby change us all. "Other-directed," then, does not mean *noblesse oblige* but true interdependence.

The norms of diversity, unity, and other-directed mutuality are precisely those that are at the core of Paul's ethics of community as it can be discerned through his letters.[16] From here, these are the features that we can see of the horizon of cruciform community when the heart of that community is power as life, love, the erotic. On the interpersonal level, they can be characterized by our practice of loving each other into being. On the institutional level, they are manifested as responsiveness; on the cultural level, they exist as hospitality. None of the three normative features can be sustained even if they can be imagined when we operate noetically and politically with power as control. Under power as control, we cannot tolerate the change that diversity brings; unity is invisible and unconvincing; the "other" is molded by our own needs to see and say and do. To use a Pauline metaphor, we simply cannot change the edifice if we leave the old foundation intact.

The norms that shape cruciform community are not new and original. They can be culled from the pages of Paul's epistles, and they are being articulated by contemporary Christian feminists. The struggles that face us in instantiating the normative contours that I have sketched are not primarily intellectual but existential. It is easy enough to *say* that Christian community should be formed around unity, diversity, and mutual upbuilding. It is easy enough to *say* that "there is neither Greek nor Jew." It is easy enough to *say* that love is at the heart of Christian community. It is a simple ethic to speak. It is an impossible ethic to live unless we believe and incorporate the power of the cross as life-giving, erotic, uncontrolled, and uncontrollable.

CONCLUSION

The argument I have mounted supports a relatively simple thesis: We will not transform our communities unless we transform our understanding and practice of power. Power takes any number of forms; power as control is real and all too familiar. However, the power of the cross, power as life, as love, as the erotic, is also real. It is God's power, and it is available to persons to experience and execute. It also forms the heart of a very old vision of Christian community that is startlingly like that being articulated by contemporary Christian feminists.

The power of the cross is not to be understood as most of the tradition has interpreted and embodied it. In distinction to traditional claims, the power of the cross does not glorify suffering but rather simply acknowledges suffering as part of life and death. The power of the cross is out of control and uncontrollable, or it becomes something else. Our intentions may be good and our will may be strong, but we cannot create enduring new forms of community by experimenting with leadership styles or new communal structures unless we base those styles and structures on power reenvisioned as I have described it. The power of the cross is not the only kind of power we encounter. We have good reason to believe that it is, however, God's power, available to us as we live it and only as we live it. We cannot think our way into it through some docetic intellectualism; practice and discourse emerge together. As it was in the first century, so it is still an experiment worth trying. "For God's foolishness is wiser than human wisdom, and God's weakness is stronger than human strength" (I Cor. 1:25).

NOTES

INTRODUCTION

1. The part that intuition and imagination play in knowledge is receiving attention from a variety of sources. See Mary Field Belenky et al., *Women's Ways of Knowing: The Development of Self, Voice and Mind* (New York: Basic Books, 1988); Sallie McFague, *Metaphorical Theology: Models of God in Religious Language* (Philadelphia: Fortress Press, 1982); William F. Lynch, S.J., *Images of Hope: Imagination as Healer of the Hopeless* (Baltimore: Helicon, 1965). The very concept of "pure rationality" is being challenged by many forms of postmodernist thought.

2. I am alluding to a fundamental feature of what Heidegger and those following him call the *Lebenswelt*, a concept similar in function to Clifford Geertz's understanding of culture in his *Interpretation of Cultures* (New York: Basic Books, 1973).

3. James Gustafson refers to the phrase "human flourishing" as a "weasel term." He disparages it as being empty of content. In a sense, he is right, for the real work of substantive ethics is to specify the content of "human flourishing." On the other hand, it is a useful phrase by which to articulate the goals of human community and communal ethics. Not all ethics are centered around the goal of human flourishing; Gustafson's work is an example.

4. This broadly sketched picture and that which follows is based largely on the historical research of Elisabeth Schüssler-Fiorenza and Wayne Meeks as well as on my own reading of early Christian history.

5. See Elisabeth Schüssler-Fiorenza's historical reconstruction in her *In Memory of Her: A Feminist Theological Reconstruction of Christian Origins* (New York: Crossroad, 1983).

6. I put the *es* in parentheses because the individual denominations are not radically different at this point.

7. For example, white Christian feminists have exposed and continue to expose the depth and extent of racism in our communities and in our scholarship.

8. See Katie Cannon's discussion of the role of black women's experience in the development of her womanist ethics and her analysis of the ways in which black women's literature functions in foundationally normative ways in *Black Womanist Ethics* (Atlanta: Scholars Press, 1988).

9. See Joanne Carlson Brown and Carole R. Bohn, eds., *Christianity, Patriarchy, and Abuse: A Feminist Critique* (New York: The Pilgrim Press, 1990).

101

10. I will discuss some of the negative effects of the cross in chapters 1 and 5.

11. See Susan Faludi, *Backlash: The Undeclared War Against American Women* (New York: Crown, 1991).

12. See Elizabeth Janeway, *Powers of the Weak* (New York: Knopf, 1980); Dorothee Soelle, *The Strength of the Weak: Toward a Christian Feminist Identity,* trans. Robert Kimber and Rita Kimber (Philadelphia: Westminster Press, 1984).

1. ONE FACE OF POWER: POWER AS CONTROL

1. Letty M. Russell, *Household of Freedom: Authority in Feminist Theology* (Philadelphia: Westminster Press, 1987), p. 21.

2. See Iris Marion Young, *Justice and the Politics of Difference* (Princeton, N.J.: Princeton University Press, 1990); Catherine MacKinnon, *Feminism Unmodified: Discourse on Life and Law* (Cambridge, Mass.: Harvard University Press, 1988).

3. Some Christian theological convictions—for example, the Calvinist doctrine of double predestination—would seem to argue against this claim. Even in that case, however, whatever inequalities of merit and grace may obtain are hidden in the mind of God and therefore not accessible to human discernment. Thus they cannot function as a basis for human behavior.

4. Gene Outka, *Agape: An Ethical Analysis* (New Haven, Conn.: Yale University Press, 1972).

5. A number of historical studies are both interesting and valuable. (I am not drawing upon the extensive literature being generated by contemporary Wicca movement(s), though it is very interesting.) Among the studies dealing with continental European witchcraft are: Valerie I. J. Flint, *The Rise of Magic in Early Medieval Europe* (Princeton, N.J.: Princeton University Press, 1991); Charles Alva Hoyt, *Witchcraft* (Carbondale: Southern Illinois University Press, 1981); Christina Larner, *Witchcraft and Religion: The Politics of Popular Belief* (Oxford, England: Basil Blackwell, 1984); G. R. Quaifek, *Godly Zeal and Furious Rage: The Witch in Early Modern Europe* (New York: St. Martin's Press, 1987); and Geoffrey Scarre, *Witchcraft and Magic in Sixteenth- and Seventeenth-Century Europe* (Atlantic Highlands, N.J.: Humanities Press International, Inc., 1987). Other medieval documents available in modern translation include Pierre-François Fournier, *Magie et Sorcellerie: essai historique accompagné des documents concernant la Magie et la Sorcellerie en Auvergne* (Moulins: Éditions Ipomée, 1977); Brother Francesco Maria Guazzo, *Compendium Maleficarum,* ed. Montague Summers, trans. E. A. Ashwin (London: John Rodker, 1929); Johann Weyer, *De praestigiis daemonum: Witches, Devils and Doctors in the Renaissance,* trans. John Shea (Binghamton, N.Y.: Medieval and Renaissance Texts and Studies, 1991).

6. See Peter Berger and Thomas Luckmann, *The Social Construction of Reality: A Treatise in the Sociology of Knowledge* (Garden City, N.Y.: Doubleday, 1966).

7. See the studies cited above.

8. Henricus Institoris and Jakob Sprenger, *Malleus Maleficarum,* trans. and ed., Montague Summers (New York: R. Blom, 1948, 1970). There is some debate about the extent of the actual use of this document as a manual; its influence, however, is undisputed. Its value for our purposes is the window it provides through which we can see the structures and uses of power in the process of identifying and persecuting witches.

9. Ibid., p. 272.

10. In this regard it is interesting to note that a large part of the activity of witches had to do with the sexual functioning of males. See ibid., pp. 172ff.

11. See ibid., p. 181.

12. See ibid., p. 194.

13. The misogyny of the document is no less horrible because it is so blatant. The authors identify the intellectual and spiritual weakness of women as contributing to their greater gullibility to the devil. And they write, "But the natural reason is that she is more carnal than a man, as is clear from her many carnal abominations." (Institoris and Sprenger, *Malleus Maleficarum*, p. 121). And "her carnal nature" is discussed by the celibate male authors in prurient detail.

14. *Malleus Maleficarum*, abridged, ed., with introduction by Pennethorne Hughes (London: Folio Society, 1968), p. 48.

15. Ibid., p. 50.

16. Ibid., p. 60.

17. Though not all persons convicted of witchcraft were women, the vast majority were, so I follow the practice of the authors of the *Malleus Maleficarum* and use exclusively female pronouns when referring to witches.

18. *Malleus Maleficarum*, p. 214.

19. The document recommends starting with "gentle torture" and increasing its severity if her testimony continues to be unsatisfactory. See ibid., p. 218.

20. Ibid., pp. 231-32.

21. I am contrasting the position of the author of Ephesians with that of Paul's understanding of the power of the cross. Implied in my use of the biblical materials is the conviction based on both historical and theological evidence that the pseudo-Pauline epistles contradicted Paul's understanding of power as exemplified in I Corinthians.

22. Scholars are divided over the authorship of Ephesians. Andrew Lincoln summarizes the arguments against Paul's having written the letter in *Ephesians,* Word Biblical Commentary #42 (Dallas: Word Books, 1990). Markus Barth argues for the acceptance of Paul's authorship, *The Anchor Bible, Ephesians, Introduction, Translation and Commentary on Chapters 1–3* (Garden City, N.Y.: Doubleday, 1974), pp. 36-50. I find the arguments against Paul's authorship more convincing than those for it. In either case, however, the understanding of power in Ephesians 5 is opposed to Paul's explication of the power of the cross in I Corinthians 1.

23. *The Interpreter's Bible,* Vol. X (I Corinthians, II Corinthians, Galatians, Ephesians) (Nashville: Abingdon Press, 1953); see also Lincoln, *Ephesians.*

24. The text also talks about relations between children and parents and slaves and masters, and those discussions reflect the same understanding of power as the section we are examining. There is nothing idiosyncratic about 5:21-33 in the context of the letter.

25. Like the *Malleus Maleficarum,* Ephesians assumes and reinforces the church's authority with regard to persons' relationship to God. Unlike the *Malleus Maleficarum,* Ephesians is concerned with and addressed to only those inside the walls of the church.

26. See Schüssler Fiorenza, *In Memory of Her,* for a discussion of the reversion to patriarchal marriage practices reflected in the later epistles.

27. See Susan Thistlethwaite, "Every Two Minutes: Battered Women and Feminist Interpretation," pp. 96-107 in Letty M. Russell, ed., *Feminist Interpretation of the Bible* (Philadelphia: Westminster Press, 1985).

28. See Lenore Walker, *The Battered Woman* (New York: Harper & Row, 1979), for a classic analysis of the mechanism of control in patterns of domestic violence.

29. In *Abuse and Victimization Across the Life Span* (Baltimore: The Johns Hopkins University Press, 1988) Martha Straus writes, "All victims share a profound belief in their own badness—and an underlying sense that they deserve the violence against them. The loyalty of victims of all ages to their abusers has been noted extensively in the literature on both child abuse and wife battering" (p. 3). She goes on to note that self-blame is the most difficult effect of abuse to treat.

2. THE OTHER FACE OF POWER: POWER AS LIFE

1. See note 1 to the Introduction.

2. Audre Lorde, *Sister Outsider: Essays and Speeches by Audre Lorde* (Trumansburg, N.Y.: The Crossing Press, 1984). The essay was first given as an address in 1978.

3. Any feminist is marginalized by contemporary Christian communities; an openly lesbian Christian is pushed even further to the edges. Of course, if one defines the center differently, the margins appear in different places as well, and for Christian feminists, Heyward's work is indeed central.

4. Brown and Bohn, *Christianity, Patriarchy, and Abuse.*

5. I would argue that his understanding of power is in harmony with that represented in the stories about Jesus in the Gospels, but his discussion is conceptually more accessible because it is more explicit.

6. My discussion will present only the skeleton of Heyward's discussion, omitting and thus not doing justice to the poetry and passion of her work.

7. Carter Heyward, *Touching Our Strength: The Erotic as Power and the Love of God* (San Francisco: Harper & Row, 1989), p. 24.

8. In the next chapter I will raise the issue of the adequacy of her fundamentally interpersonal understanding of justice for an overall conception of power and justice on a societal level.

9. Equality is an important feature of right relationships, but inequality is not incompatible with justice, depending on the nature and purpose of the inequality. For example, adult/child relationships may be just if the inequality is understood to be temporary and in service of the growth and development of the child. Inequality does *not* necessitate a relationship of dominance and submission, though our society often acts as if it does. See Heyward, *Touching Our Strength,* p. 35.

10. Beverly Harrison, *Making the Connections: Essays in Feminist Social Ethics,* ed. Carol S. Robb (Boston: Beacon Press, 1985), p. 12.

11. Heyward, *Touching Our Strength,* p. 56.

12. See Sharon Welch, *A Feminist Ethic of Risk* (Minneapolis: Fortress Press, 1990).

13. Heyward, *Touching Our Strength,* p. 58.

14. See the introduction in Toril Moi, ed., *The Kristeva Reader* (New York: Columbia University Press, 1986).

15. I do not see Kristeva moving as far away from Freud as some of her interpreters think, or perhaps as she herself thinks. See Moi, ibid. I am impressed by her analysis of Freud's gender blindness, but I wonder how free of it she is since the concepts of "the maternal" and "the Father" seem much more primitive and universal than a radical historical constructionist could tolerate.

16. See, for example, Mary Field Belenky et al., *Women's Ways of Knowing: The Develop-*

ment of Self, Voice and Mind (New York: Basic Books, Inc., 1986), and Carol Gilligan's work. "The symbolic" may also find echoes in nonfeminist postmodernist thought, but it is not the subject of this study.

17. Sigmund Freud, *Civilization and Its Discontents,* trans. James Strachey (New York: W. W. Norton & Co., 1961).

18. Part of the clue for me that Kristeva has not moved as far from Freud as she claims is her identification of lesbianism and psychosis. For her, lesbians have transgressed their primary identification with the mother and have identified with the father in desiring the mother. See Judith Butler, "The Body Politics of Julia Kristeva," in Nancy Fraser and Sandra Lee Bartky, eds., *Revaluing French Feminism: Critical Essays on Difference, Agency and Culture* (Bloomington: Indiana University Press), p. 169. Also see Moi, *The Kristeva Reader,* p. 149. Thus she has no interpretive tools by which to assess lesbianism as a healthy human state.

19. Susan J. Hekman, *Gender and Knowledge: Elements of a Postmodern Feminism* (Boston: Northeastern University Press, 1990), p. 90.

20. Butler, "The Body Politics of Julia Kristeva," p. 163.

21. In *The Journal of Feminist Studies in Religion* 8, 1 (Spring 1992), Kathleen Sands argues against what she sees as the idealization of eros and sexuality in feminist thought, and she critiques Heyward among others in that regard. However, in making that argument, Sands conflates "the erotic" with genital sexuality. "The erotic" as Lorde and then Heyward and I use the term may encompass sexuality but is not encompassed by it. Eroticism is a broader category than sex narrowly understood, and it includes all forms of embodied connectedness that are life-giving. There is a kind of ethical circularity in our use of the term, since we do posit erotic experience as life-giving and life-giving experience as erotic. That circularity, however, is in service of the evocation of a whole level of human experience that is remote for most of us and almost inaccessible to some of us. I argue that the erotic is more familiar to women than to men because of our cultural socialization, but it is not characteristic of most articulations of white, middle-income experience in general. Whether this use of the concept of eroticism is helpful to the debate over sexual behavior that is underway in the "secular" feminist community is an issue I cannot address here.

22. Audre Lorde, *Sister Outsider: Essays and Speeches by Audre Lorde* (Trumansburg, N.Y.: The Crossing Press, 1984), pp. 56-57.

23. It is interesting to read the two creation accounts in Genesis in the light of this discussion. The first account stresses unity, the second gender division. The second has been far more oppressive to women.

24. See Nancy Fraser, "The Uses and Abuses of French Discourse Theories for Feminist Politics" in Fraser and Bartky, *Revaluing French Feminism,* p. 183.

25. See Sally B. Purvis, "Problems and Possibilities in Paul's Ethics of Community," unpublished dissertation, Yale University, 1987.

26. Ibid.

27. We may recall here the debate in New Testament scholarship about whether certain groups in the Corinthian community were gnostics or protognostics. Based on the textual evidence from I Corinthians, we need not posit a heresy or a protoheresy; rival factions based on rival loyalties to different leaders strikes me as simply human.

28. For an extended and eloquent treatment of the theme of "reversal," see Allen Verhey, *The Great Reversal: Ethics and the New Testament* (Grand Rapids: Eerdmans, 1984), pp. 106ff.

29. From the confrontations with Pharaoh and with Baal to the imagery of Revelation, there are many instances of biblical portrayals of God's power as force and control.

30. The term *Christian* is a later designation for the followers of Jesus Christ and therefore never appears in the Pauline corpus. However, it is certainly appropriate to the communities Paul founded, and its familiarity and convenience make it virtually indispensible for my discussion.

31. See also Romans 8:37-39.

32. I understand Paul's passion for "his gospel" to be motivated not simply by his need for credibility in the communities he founded but more important by his conviction that "the gospel" would be lost to the world if the communities did not embody the power of the cross but rather reverted to power as control. That, of course, is exactly what happened. My reading of Paul stands in contradiction to that of Elizabeth Castelli, *Imitating Paul: A Discourse of Power* (Louisville: Westminster/John Knox Press, 1991).

3. FOUR DIMENSIONS OF POWER

1. Beverly Harrison frames her theological ethics in the context of connectedness. See Harrison, *Making the Connections.*

2. It can be argued that a definitive analysis of human experience is itself oppressive, since all analyses are perspective-dependent and therefore only definitive within a certain context.

3. See Janeway, *Powers of the Weak,* for a detailed analysis of this phenomenon. Aristophanes' *Lysistrata* is a classic, powerful, and wonderfully amusing dramatization of "the powers of the weak" with its ancient depiction of female pacifism. See Aristophanes, *Lysistrata,* ed. with introduction and commentary by Jeffrey Henderson (New York: Oxford University Press, 1987).

4. See James Newton Poling, *The Abuse of Power: A Theological Problem* (Nashville: Abingdon Press, 1991) for an excellent discussion of child sexual abuse as a manifestation of evil power. He writes, "Abuse of power for the individual is motivated by fear and by the resulting desire to control the power of life. This fear and arrogance are then used to create societies in which structures of domination create special possibilities for the privileged at the expense of shared power for all persons" (p. 27). I depart from Poling's analysis when he identifies the nature of God's power as ambiguous, as potentially life-giving *and* destructive. See ibid., p. 177.

5. See Sara Ruddick, *Maternal Thinking: Toward a Politics of Peace* (Boston: Beacon Press, 1989).

6. See H. Richard Niebuhr, *The Responsible Self: An Essay in Christian Moral Philosophy* (New York: Harper and Bros., 1963).

7. Beverly Harrison, "The Power of Anger in the Work of Love," in *Making the Connections: Essays in Feminist Social Ethics,* ed. Carol S. Robb (Boston: Beacon Press, 1985), p. 11. In the lives and careers of all of us we encounter specific writings that quite unexpectedly affect our understanding and shape our thought in fundamental ways. This essay by Harrison has functioned that way for me.

8. I have no particular investment in separating intellectual, emotional, and spiritual capacities. I would be happy to use the term *spirit* alone. I use the multiple terms only to evoke the widest possible sense of personhood.

9. It goes without saying that a lot of what we call "sport" is not especially playful.

10. Iris Marion Young, *Justice and the Politics of Difference.*

11. Ibid., p. 9.

12. Richard Sennett discusses paternalism as an "authority of false love." His is an interesting analysis of fathers and the mechanism of control, though he does not use that terminology. Richard Sennett, *Authority* (New York: Knopf, 1980).

13. Judaism is no more oppressive of women than is Christianity, if one can even quantify such an issue at all. In any case, both have misognyist elements in their histories and theologies, and both have liberating features.

14. Letty M. Russell, *Household of Freedom*, p. 17.

15. Beverly Harrison, *Our Right to Choose: Toward a New Ethic of Abortion* (Boston: Beacon Press, 1983), p. 99.

16. Paul Ricoeur, "Biblical Hermeneutics," *Semeia* IV (1975).

17. In the context of postmodern consciousness, the issue of "the subject" is widely debated by feminist scholars. Jean Grimshaw presents a feminist anthropology that integrates the relationality and the autonomy of personhood. See her *Philosophy and Feminist Thinking* (Minneapolis: University of Minnesota Press, 1986).

18. See Clifford Geertz, *Interpretation of Cultures* (New York: Basic Books, 1973).

19. See, for example, the essays in *Feminism & Foucault: Reflections on Resistance*, eds. Irene Diamond and Lee Quinby (Boston: Northeastern University Press, 1988).

20. Foucault himself may not have been entirely consistent with regard to the issue of personal identity. Interpretations of his writings certainly vary.

21. See Faludi, *Backlash.*

22. For a classic discussion of the phenomenon of cognitive dissonance, see Berger and Luckmann, *The Social Construction of Reality.*

23. Carol Gilligan and other feminist psychologists and philosophers have exposed the blatant male bias of culturally formative theories of "man." A culture of life cannot accept as its formative myth without reservation or modification the theory of a man who was never able to answer the question "What do women want?"

24. Identifying and developing those images have been central concerns of Christian feminists from the beginning of this wave and, to some degree, the last. See, for example, McFague, *Metaphorical Theology.*

4. THE POWER OF THE CROSS

1. This is, of course, a controversial claim and one that a biblical fundamentalist cannot accept. I do not simply claim that the biblical portrayal of God is complex, but that not all its facets cohere. Given my arguments about the nature of God's power, outright rejection of some biblical images and narratives is necessary.

2. Anyone who wants to argue for a different concept of God's power from the one Paul presents would have scriptural resources to do so but would not be able to ignore Paul's claims. Crucifixion is itself an argument against control. If we take seriously the power of the cross, there is a way in which the Christian story forces a decisive choice among options presented in the New Testament, though Christian theology by and large has not used the power of the cross as a hermeneutical principle.

3. Whether Paul underwent an actual conversion and the subsequent nature of his relation to Judaism are related controversies in New Testament scholarship. While they are interesting and important issues, their resolution does not directly affect this discussion.

4. The literature on the social phenomenon of resocialization is vast. In addition to the texts by Berger and Luckmann, Clifford Geertz, and Wayne Meeks already cited, see David A. Goslin, *A Handbook of Socialization Theory and Research* (Chicago: Rand McNally, 1969), for a classic statement of the process.

5. See Berger and Luckmann, *The Social Construction of Reality;* Goslin, *A Handbook of Socialization Theory and Research.*

6. Wayne Meeks, *The First Urban Christians: The Social World of the Apostle Paul* (New Haven, Conn.: Yale University Press, 1983).

7. In *Imitating Paul: A Discourse of Power* (Louisville: Westminster/John Knox Press, 1991), Elizabeth A. Castelli argues that mimesis in Paul's letters functions as a conservative, even controlling, strategy. Though she alludes to a new interpretation of power that is being introduced in his texts (p. 38, e.g.), she never seriously considers what that "new interpretation of power" might be and how it might function to modify or even transform the mimetic heritage within which Paul was operating. Rather, she assumes a concept of power as control and uses it to argue that through the power in his texts Paul at least aspired to control.

8. Scholars dispute the degree and places of overlap between the Judeo/Greco-Roman "world," which itself was far from hegemonic, and the nature of the developing Christian ethos. Whatever novelty one may find in the Christian communities, it is indubitable that many features of daily life were simply imported from the cultural experiences and expectations of the members. It is only when the former culture clashes with at least Paul's version of the "new" one that we can see the process of resocialization at work. See I Corinthians 11:17-22.

9. See Peter Berger, *The Sacred Canopy: Elements of a Sociological Theory of Religion* (Garden City, N.Y.: Doubleday, 1969).

10. See the discussion by J. P. M. Walsh, S.J., *The Mighty from Their Thrones: Power in the Biblical Tradition* (Philadelphia: Fortress Press, 1987), p. 155. Walsh does not address the explicit distinction between kinds of power that I am making, but his description of the nature and function of the cross in relationship to violence supports my distinction.

11. The rampant docetism of our Christian culture was dramatically exhibited by the reaction to the movie *The Last Temptation of Christ* and the outcry over the depiction of Jesus' sexual desire. African-American churches seem to be less tempted by the docetic option, though there may be problems with his sexuality. See Jacquelyn Grant, *White Women's Christ and Black Women's Jesus: Feminist Christology and Womanist Response* (Atlanta: Scholars Press, 1989).

12. I am not suggesting that Paul would use this language, or even agree with it. I am saying that it is a conclusion we can draw from the rest of what he says.

13. Paul responded to questions about individual life after death; see I Thessalonians 4 and I Corinthians 15. Paul, however, emphasized the nature of human community shaped by the presence and the power of the risen Christ. See, for example, I Corinthians 12 and Galatians 6.

14. Paul does not distinguish between building up individuals and building up the community; they happen together. He never even considers a conflict between individual and communal needs. See Purvis, "Problems and Possibilities in Paul's Ethics of Community."

15. See, for example, Romans 14, I Corinthians 12–13, II Corinthians 8, Galatians 5.

16. We know from Paul's letter to the Galatians that Christian leaders were not unanimous regarding the rejection of dietary laws from the Christian cult. Paul's perspective, at least in this regard, seems to have prevailed.

17. See Purvis, "Problems and Possibilities in Paul's Ethics of Community."

5. RECLAIMING THE CROSS

1. I find their critique of the liberationist position unconvincing. Recognizing the inevitability of suffering strikes me as an essentially different response, both morally and affectively, from glorifying it.

2. Heyward, *Touching Our Strength,* p. 115. Brown and Parker critique Heyward's earlier treatment of the cross, but since their critique proceeds by way of rhetorical questions, it is not substantively clear what their objections are. I read them as in fundamental agreement.

3. Ibid.

4. It is interesting to note in this regard that Paul's letter to the community at Rome contains almost no discussion of the power of the cross, whereas the correspondence with the communities he founded and/or helped to shape is replete with it. His understanding of the power of God as something radically new, is the basis from which his parenaesis emanates. It is at the heart of his project of resocializing persons into the new life with Christ.

5. In *Sacred Violence: Paul's Hermeneutic of the Cross* (Minneapolis: Fortress Press, 1992), Robert G. Hammerton-Kelly uses a Girardian hermeneutic to argue that eros, desire itself, necessarily creates rivalry and the need for a scapegoat. According to Hammerton-Kelly's analysis, the revelation of the cross is that it undermines the inevitable jealousy and lust created by the prohibitions of the law by having God be the scapegoat, the victim of violence. Hammerton-Kelly accepts and employs Nygren's distinction between eros and agape, and he understands power to be essentially violent. He never entertains the possibility that desire and power themselves could be understood and experienced in other ways. It is precisely the assumptions with which Hammerton-Kelly operates that this and other feminist analyses are meant to challenge.

6. The deeply experiential grounding of Paul's ethics is the best argument against any attempt to gnosticize Paul.

7. See Purvis, "Problems and Possibilities in Paul's Ethics of Community," for the argument that Paul's references to boasting are evidence he invokes that he is living by, and recommending, a new value system, one that cannot be extracted from the values of either Jewish or Greco-Roman culture. I argue that he is not recommending suffering for its own sake but rather encourages enduring it as the inevitable price for living by standards that the larger culture rejects.

8. Marcia Riggs argues that the integrity of the community, male and female, is essential for womanist ethics (in class discussion at Columbia Theological Seminary, Decatur, Georgia, Spring 1992). It may be that there is a difference between white women and women of color in this regard. In other words, separatism may carry different moral weight for white women and women of color, given the different levels of power held by white men and men of color. Marcia Riggs and other womanists have argued against separatism on racial grounds. However, for white women, separatism is at least a possible strategy, if not a viable long-range goal.

9. These claims do not in and of themselves constitute an adequate argument for Christian pacifism, though they do lend that position some support. They do, however, undergird the presumption against violence and require that all violence be justified. Whether something like just war theory provides adequate justification is too complex a question to treat here.

10. See Brown and Bohn, *Christianity, Patriarchy, and Abuse,* p. 27.

11. I believe that insight was at the heart of Paul's itinerate evangelism and at the center of his ethical teaching.

12. It may be a helpful reminder to note here that feminist Christians may be male or female.

13. Nancy Fraser, *Unruly Practices: Power, Discourse, and Gender in Contemporary Social Theory* (Minneapolis: University of Minnesota Press, 1989), chap. 8, "Struggle over Needs: Outline of a Socialist-Feminist Critical Theory of Late Capitalist Political Culture."

14. Ibid., p. 175.

15. Rebecca Chopp, *The Power to Speak: Feminism, Language, God* (New York: Crossroad, 1989), p. 124.

16. See Purvis, "Problems and Possibilities in Paul's Ethics of Community."

FURTHER READING

Aristophanes. *Lysistrata*. Edited by Jeffrey Henderson. New York: Oxford University Press, 1990.

Barth, Markus. *Ephesians*. The Anchor Bible. Garden City, N.Y.: Doubleday, 1974.

Belenky, Mary Field, et al. *Women's Ways of Knowing: The Development of Self, Voice, and Mind*. New York: Basic Books, 1988.

Berger, Peter. *The Sacred Canopy: Elements of a Sociological Theory of Religion*. Garden City, N.Y.: Doubleday and Company, Inc., 1969.

Bergman, Peter, and Thomas Luckmann. *The Social Construction of Reality: A Treatise in the Sociology of Knowledge*. Garden City, N.Y.: Doubleday, 1966.

Brown, Joanne Carlson, and Carole R. Bohn, eds. *Christianity, Patriarchy, and Abuse: A Feminist Critique*. New York: The Pilgrim Press, 1989.

Butler, Judith. "The Body Politics of Julia Kristeva." In *Revaluing French Feminism: Critical Essays on Difference, Agency and Culture*. Edited by Nancy Fraser and Sandra Lee Bartky. Bloomington: Indiana University Press, 1992.

Cannon, Katie. *Black Womanist Ethics*. Atlanta: Scholars Press, 1988.

Castelli, Elizabeth. *Imitating Paul: A Discourse of Power*. Louisville: Westminster/John Knox Press, 1991.

Chopp, Rebecca. *The Power to Speak: Feminism, Language, God*. New York: Crossroad, 1989.

Diamond, Irene, and Lee Quinby, eds. *Feminism and Foucault: Reflections on Resistance*. Boston: Northeastern University Press, 1988.

Faludi, Susan. *Backlash: The Undeclared War Against American Women*. New York: Crown, 1991.

Farley, Margaret. *Personal Commitments: Beginning, Keeping, Changing.* San Francisco: Harper & Row, 1986.

Flint, Valerie I. J. *The Rise of Magic in Early Medieval Europe.* Princeton: Princeton University Press, 1991.

Fournier, Pierre François. *Magie et Sorcellerie: essai historique accompagné des documents concernant la Magie et la Sorcellerie en Auvergne.* Moulins: Editions Ipomée, 1977.

Fraser, Nancy. "The Uses and Abuses of French Discourse Theories for Feminist Politics." In *Revaluing French Feminism: Critical Essays on Difference, Agency and Culture.* Edited by Nancy Fraser and Sandra Lee Bartky. Bloomington: Indiana University Press, 1992.

_____. *Unruly Practices: Power, Discourse, and Gender in Contemporary Social Theory.* Minneapolis: University of Minnesota Press, 1989.

Freud, Sigmund. *Civilization and Its Discontents.* Translated by James Strachey. New York: W. W. Norton and Co., 1963.

Geertz, Clifford. *Interpretation of Cultures.* New York: Basic Books, 1973.

Goslin, David A. *A Handbook of Socialization Theory and Research.* Chicago: Rand McNally, 1969.

Grant, Jacquelyn. *White Women's Christ and Black Women's Jesus: Feminist Christology and Womanist Response.* Atlanta: Scholars Press, 1989.

Grimshaw, Jean. *Philosophy and Feminist Thinking.* Minneapolis: University of Minnesota Press, 1986.

Guazzo, Brother Francesco Maria. *Compendium Maleficarum.* Translated by E. A. Ashwin. Edited by Montague Summers. London: John Rodker, 1929.

Hammerton-Kelly, Robert G. *Sacred Violence: Paul's Hermeneutic of the Cross.* Minneapolis: Fortress Press, 1992.

Harrison, Beverly. *Making the Connections: Essays in Feminist Social Ethics.* Edited by Carol S. Robb. Boston: Beacon Press, 1985.

_____. *Our Right to Choose: Toward a New Ethic of Abortion.* Boston: Beacon Press, 1983.

Heyward, Carter. *Our Passion for Justice: Images of Power, Sexuality, and Liberation.* New York: Pilgrim Press, 1984.

_____. *The Redemption of God: A Theology of Mutual Relation.* Washington, D.C.: University Press of America, 1982.

_____. *Revolutionary Forgiveness: Feminist Reflections on Nicaragua.* Maryknoll, N.Y.: Orbis Books, 1987.

_____. *Touching Our Strength: The Erotic as Power and the Love of God.* San Francisco: Harper & Row, 1989.

Heyward, Carter, and Ellen C. Davis. *Speaking of Christ: A Lesbian Feminist Voice.* New York: Pilgrim Press, 1989.

Hoyt, Charles Alva. *Witchcraft.* Carbondale: Southern Illinois University Press, 1989.

Institoris, Henricus, and Jakob Sprenger. *Malleus Maleficarum.* Translated and edited by Montague Summers. New York: R. Blom, 1948, 1970.

The Interpreter's Bible. Vol. X. I Corinthians, II Corinthians, Galatians, Ephesians. Nashville: Abingdon Press, 1953.

Janeway, Elizabeth. *Powers of the Weak.* New York: Knopf, 1980.

Kraemer, Heinrich, Jakob Sprenger, and Pennethorne Hughes. *Malleus Maleficarum,* abridged. London: Folio Society, 1968.

Kristeva, Julia. *About Chinese Women.* New York: Urizen Books, 1977.

_____. *Desire in Language: A Semiotic Approach to Literature and Art.* New York: Columbia University Press, 1980.

_____, et al. *Essays in Semiotics. Approaches to Semiotics.* Vol. 4. The Hague: Mouton, 1971.

_____. *In the Beginning Was Love: Psychoanalysis and Faith.* European Perspectives. New York: Columbia University Press, 1988.

_____. *Powers of Horror: An Essay on Abjection.* European Perspectives. New York: Columbia University Press, 1984.

_____. *Revolution in Poetic Language.* New York: Columbia University Press, 1984.

_____. *Tales of Love.* New York: Columbia University Press, 1987.

Larner, Christina. *Witchcraft and Religion: The Politics of Popular Belief.* Oxford, England: Basil Blackwell, 1984.

Lincoln, Andrew. *Ephesians.* Word Biblical Commentary, No. 42. Dallas: Word Books, 1990.

Lorde, Audre. *Sister Outsider: Essays and Speeches by Audre Lorde.* Trumansburg, N.Y.: The Crossing Press, 1984.

Lynch, William F., S. J. *Images of Hope: Imagination as Healer of the Hopeless.* Baltimore: Helicon, 1965.

McFague, Sallie. *Metaphorical Theology: Models of God in Religious Language.* Philadelphia: Augsburg Fortress Press, 1982.

MacKinnon, Catherine. *Feminism Unmodified: A Discourse on Life and Law.* Cambridge, Mass.: Harvard University Press, 1987.

Meeks, Wayne. *The First Urban Christians: The Social World of the Apostle Paul.* New Haven: Yale University Press, 1983.

Moi, Toril, ed. *A Kristeva Reader.* New York: Columbia University Press, 1986.

Niebuhr, H. Richard. *The Responsible Self: An Essay in Christian Moral Philosophy.* New York: Harper and Row, 1978.

Outka, Gene. *Agape: An Ethical Analysis.* New Haven: Yale University Press, 1972.

Poling, James Newton. *The Abuse of Power: A Theological Problem.* Nashville: Abingdon Press, 1991.

Purvis, Sally B. "Problems and Possibilities in Paul's Ethics of Community." Unpublished dissertation. Yale University, 1987.

Quaifex, G. R. *Godly Zeal and Furious Rage: The Witch in Early Modern Europe.* New York: St. Martin's Press, 1987.

Ricoeur, Paul. "Biblical Hermeneutics." *Semeia* IV. 1975.

Robb, Carol, ed. "The Power of Anger in the Work of Love." In *Making the Connections: Essays in Feminist Social Ethics.* Boston: Beacon Press, 1985.

Ruddick, Sara. *Maternal Thinking: Toward a Politics of Peace.* Boston: Ballantine Books, 1990.

Russell, Letty M. *Changing Contexts of Our Faith.* Philadelphia: Fortress Press, 1985.

_____. *The Church with AIDS: Renewal in the Midst of Crisis.* Louisville: Westminster/John Knox Press, 1990.

_____. *Feminist Interpretation of the Bible.* Philadelphia: Westminster Press, 1985.

_____. *The Future of Partnership.* Philadelphia: Westminster Press, 1979.

_____. *Growth in Partnership.* Philadelphia: Westminster Press, 1981.

_____. *Household of Freedom: Authority in Feminist Theology.* Philadelphia: Westminster Press, 1987.

_____. *Human Liberation in a Feminist Perspective—A Theology.* Philadelphia: Westminster Press, 1974.

_____. *Inheriting Our Mothers' Gardens: Feminist Theology in Third World Perspective.* Philadelphia: Westminster Press, 1988.

Sands, Kathleen. "Use of the Thea(o)logian: Sex and Theodicy in Religious Feminism." *The Journal of Feminist Studies in Religion* 8, 1 (Spring 1992).

Scarre, Geoffrey. *Witchcraft and Magic in Sixteenth- and Seventeenth-Century Europe.* Atlantic Highlands, N.J.: Humanities Press International, Inc., 1987.

Schüssler Fiorenza, Elisabeth. *Bread Not Stone: The Challenge of Feminist Biblical Interpretation.* Boston: Beacon Press, 1984.

_____. *In Memory of Her: A Feminist Theological Reconstruction of Christian Origins.* New York: Crossroad, 1983.

Sennett, Richard. *Authority.* New York: Knopf, 1980.

Soelle, Dorothee. *The Strength of the Weak: Toward a Christian Feminist Identity.*

Translated by Robert Kimber and Rita Kimber. Philadelphia: Westminster Press, 1984.

_____. *Suffering.* Translated by Everett Kalin. Philadelphia: Fortress Press, 1975.

Straus, Martha. *Abuse and Victimization Across the Life Span.* Baltimore: The Johns Hopkins University Press, 1988.

Thistlethwaite, Susan. "Every Two Minutes: Battered Women and Feminist Interpretation." In *Feminist Interpretation of the Bible.* Edited by Letty M. Russell. Philadelphia: Westminster Press, 1985.

Verhey, Allen. *The Great Reversal: Ethics and the New Testament.* Grand Rapids: Eerdmans, 1984.

Walker, Lenore. *The Battered Woman.* New York: Harper & Row, 1977.

Walsh, J. P. M., S. J. *The Mighty from Their Thrones: Power in the Biblical Tradition.* Philadelphia: Fortress Press, 1987.

Welch, Sharon. *Communities of Resistance and Solidarity: A Feminist Theology of Liberation.* Maryknoll, N.Y.: Orbis Books, 1985.

_____. *A Feminist Ethic of Risk.* Minneapolis: Fortress Press, 1990.

Weyer, Johann. *De praestigiis daemonum: Witches, Devils and Doctors in the Renaissance.* Translated by John Shea. Binghamton, N.Y.: Medieval and Renaissance Texts and Studies, 1991.

Young, Iris Marion. *Justice and the Politics of Difference.* Princeton: Princeton University Press, 1990.